AND
NOW THE
SHIPPING
FORECAST

AND

A TIDE OF

NOW THE

HISTORY AROUND

SHIPPING

OUR SHORES

FORECAST

PETER JEFFERSON

—

UIT CAMBRIDGE, ENGLAND

Published by UIT Cambridge Ltd., PO Box 145,
Cambridge CB4 1GQ, England
t / +44 1223 302 041 *w* / www.uit.co.uk

Copyright © 2011 UIT Cambridge Ltd.
Illustrations Copyright © 2011 **here.**
Designed by **here.** heredesign.co.uk
Printed in England by CPI Bookmarque

ISBN: 978-1-906860-15-8

The right of Peter Jefferson to be identified as the author of
this work has been asserted by him in accordance with the
Copyright, Designs and Patents Act 1988.

The information in this book has been included for its
instructional value. Neither the publisher nor the author
offers any warranties or representations in respect of its
fitness for a particular purpose, nor do they accept any
liability for any loss or damage arising from its use.

Many of the designations used by manufacturers and
sellers to distinguish their products are claimed as
trademarks. UIT Cambridge Ltd acknowledges trademarks
as the property of their respective owners. The Publishers
have made every effort to contact copyright owners and
if there are omissions please contact us.

10 9 8 7 6 5 4 3 2

FOR BEAU & LORENZO

PETER JEFFERSON joined the BBC in 1964. In 1969 he became an announcer and newsreader, first on the BBC World Service then across all the domestic BBC Radio networks, which included reading the Shipping Forecast for 40 years first on Radio 2 and later on Radio 4. He took early retirement in 2001 but continued working for Radio 4 in a freelance capacity until 2009 during which time he also appeared in several radio and TV programmes including plays on Radio 4 and vocally or as an actor on *EastEnders*, *Panorama*, *My Family*, *Never Mind The Buzzcocks*, *The Mighty Boosh*, *The Bill*, *Peak Practice* and *Holby City*. He currently reads the quotes on Radio 4's *Quote… Unquote*, and lives with his wife in Surrey.

ACKNOWLEDGMENTS

My thanks must go first of all to my editors **Catheryn Kilgarriff** and **Niall Mansfield** at UIT Cambridge for taking a punt in asking me to write this book, and for their patience and encouragement throughout its gestation.

Also my love and thanks to **Penny** for her patience and understanding at my long absences from family life into what I laughingly call my 'office' to write this book over the course of several months. I'm not sure what the writer's equivalent is to a golf player's 'grass widow' – but she has been 'it', and brilliantly supportive to boot.

Lastly, a big thank you to my friends and ex colleagues at both Radio 4 and Radio 2 and elsewhere for their amusing stories, some of which found their way into this volume, although others were excluded on the grounds of being far too rude. I trust you are on this list. If not, please forgive me.

Nigel Rees, David Miles, Carolyn Brown, Brian Perkins, Ken Bruce, Sean Street, Mark Beswick at the Met Office's National

Meteorological Library and Archive, **Zeb Soanes,   Carol Ann Duffy,** The Science Museum, **Gillian Clarke, Iain Purdon, Colin Berry, John Marsh, Corrie Corfield, David Willmott, Colonel R.G. Gilliat** (Retd), **MBE Admiral Sir Michael Layard** (Retd), KCB, CBE, **Robin Brodhurst, Ron Obbard, Mark Damazer** and **Gwyneth Williams.**

CONTENTS

ONE

—

PROLOGUE
15

TWO

—

THE GENESIS OF THE
SHIPPING FORECAST
23

THREE

—

NAME CHANGING BUT NOT
NAME CALLING
29

FOUR

—

THE METEOROLOGICAL
OFFICE AND THE SHIPPING
FORECAST BROADCASTS
44

FIVE

—

THE LIGHTER SIDE
64

SIX

—

UNEXPECTED OUTSIDE
BROADCAST
76

SEVEN

—

SAILING BY
81

EIGHT

—

SAILING BY THE SEAT
OF YOUR PANTS
84

NINE

—

A TALE OF SHIPPING
AREA TURBULENCE
PART ONE
94

TEN

—

A TALE OF SHIPPING
AREA TURBULENCE
PART TWO
122

ELEVEN

—

SHEDDING SOME LIGHT...
ON LIGHTHOUSES
156

TWELVE

—

CODES, CONVENTIONS
AND TRADITIONS
177

THIRTEEN

—

TIME AND GREENWICH
MEAN TIME
204

FOURTEEN

—

A LIFE ON THE OCEAN WAVE
216

FIFTEEN

—

A FINAL NOTE
221

GLOSSARY
224

SOURCES & FURTHER READING
226

INDEX
241

ONE

—

PROLOGUE

'And now the Shipping Forecast…' Over the past seven or eight decades, those words are among the most well known to emanate from wireless sets (or, later, radio sets) to listeners in the UK and its surrounding sea areas.

'There are warnings of gales in sea areas…' When I was a small boy in the late 1940s, the Shipping Forecast had already come of age, as it had reached 21 when I was but a year old. Hearing the forecasts on our rather damaged white Bakelite wireless at my home in Deal on the Kent coast is one of my earliest memories. I was much too young then to understand the Shipping Forecast's importance or relevance, let alone imagine that one day I would be reading out those words – and would continue to do so for some 40-plus years. I was far more interested in hearing *Listen With Mother*.

'The general synopsis…' Now we are firmly embedded in the 21st century, with all its technological advances. Mariners had, in fact, already been using sat nav for many years – long before we started using it in our cars. And they can now get access to the forecast by all sorts of means. So why listen to it on the rather crackly 198 long

wave on BBC Radio 4? Isn't it easier just to tap into it on the Internet whenever you so wish?

Has the Shipping Forecast lost its audience? It seems no – it has taken on an entirely new mantle. Where once it was the mainstay of fishermen and all other shipping traffic around not just our shores but right down to Portugal, southern Spain and parts of north Africa, it has also gained over the decades many new listeners – the bulk of whom have never set to sea except perhaps on a short Channel ferry crossing. Late at night, before Radio 4 hands over to the BBC World Service, it has become something of a 'must hear' before the cloak of sleep envelops the listening public.

SO WHERE ACTUALLY ARE ALL THE SHIPPING AREAS THAT YOU HEAR ABOUT?

—

As you can see on the adjacent map, the areas start in the north east with Viking and the Utsires, then follow the east coast of Scotland and England, along the English Channel, and down to Biscay, FitzRoy and Trafalgar off the French, Spanish and Portuguese coasts. Heading north again, through Sole, they spread around both sides of the island of Ireland and end with Fair Isle, Faeroes and South East Iceland in the north west. So you can see clearly that a wind blowing from the north west comes straight from Iceland to the UK, usually bringing colder weather – along with clouds of volcanic ash whenever an Icelandic volcano decides to blow its stack.

The area forecasts for the next 24 hours…' Despite most people not knowing much about the shipping areas or what the forecasts really mean, many have been touched by the Shipping Forecast's unusual

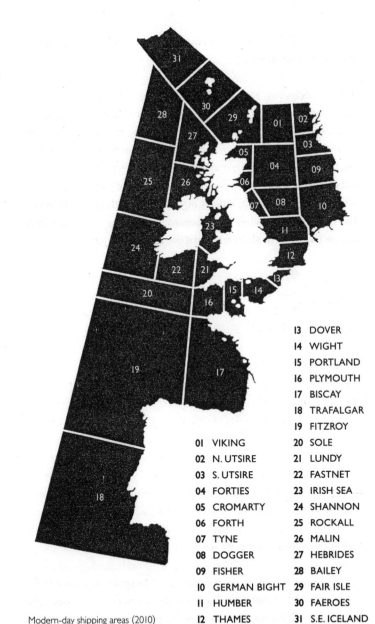

13	DOVER
14	WIGHT
15	PORTLAND
16	PLYMOUTH
17	BISCAY
18	TRAFALGAR
19	FITZROY
01 VIKING	20 SOLE
02 N. UTSIRE	21 LUNDY
03 S. UTSIRE	22 FASTNET
04 FORTIES	23 IRISH SEA
05 CROMARTY	24 SHANNON
06 FORTH	25 ROCKALL
07 TYNE	26 MALIN
08 DOGGER	27 HEBRIDES
09 FISHER	28 BAILEY
10 GERMAN BIGHT	29 FAIR ISLE
11 HUMBER	30 FAEROES
12 THAMES	31 S.E. ICELAND

Modern-day shipping areas (2010)

litany of facts and figures. It has also been easy game for comedic treatment – for instance Eccles in *The Goon Show* did 'winds light to variable' for his BBC announcer's audition – and it has been used by various pop groups and film-makers. It has inspired poems by Carol Ann Duffy, the Poet Laureate, Gillian Clarke, the former National Poet of Wales, and Sean Street to name but three who have thrown in their hats. It has without doubt permeated the British psyche in a most extraordinary way.

When Mark Damazer, the former controller of Radio 4, was asked if he could see the removal of this radio institution, he said in effect that in spite of many other ways of getting hold of the information, the four Radio 4 forecasts each day might just save someone's life, and meanwhile, he had high regard for its intrinsic and ever-widening appeal to listeners the length and breadth of the UK and beyond – such is the range of the long wave transmitter. The fact that most people have no idea what it all means seems to matter not a jot!

SO, WHERE TO START IN THIS 'EVERYDAY STORY OF MARINER FOLK'?

—

Unlike nowadays, once the fishing industry was not in peril of running out of stock or being strangled by EU legislation, but the brave men who went to sea to supply the nation with readily available and nutritious food took huge risks – and often still do – especially in some of the more treacherous waters, where weather conditions can change suddenly. How to help them make their lives safer was the question posed.

Various means for transmitting forecast bulletins to fishing boats were tried in the early 20th century – more on these in the next chapter – but in the 1920s the BBC became involved.

On November 14th, 1922, the BBC broadcast its first weather forecast, using telegraphy and BBC Transmitters and two years later it began the daily broadcast for shipping that, despite changes in format, frequency and indeed to some extent content, was very much the forecast that we are still all familiar with today. In the 1920s the BBC was still in its infancy, but Lord Reith and Co. quickly realised that this new-fangled means of educating, informing and entertaining the general public was catching on fast. Daily listening figures could reach 15 million, levels hard to imagine even in TV terms these days. So rapid advances were being made to widen coverage, and in 1925 a brand new long wave transmitter at Daventry began broadcasting the National Service, in which the news of the day was reported in a completely impartial fashion; it reached about 94% of the UK's population! In 1934 the even more powerful Droitwich transmitter took over. This one is still working today, although is getting rather old now and has been known to 'fall over', but it still carries the Shipping Forecast far and wide.

Another early problem was how to compile the forecasts, from collecting and collating information from the manned coastal waters stations (they are automatic now) to getting that information to the BBC. There were different Government departments involved of course, all of whom had to agree on formats and protocols – yes, there was plenty of red tape around then too and many of these emerging departments were jostling for position hoping to inflict pre-emptive strikes on other Whitehall mandarins. Some things don't change, do they?

Communications were nothing like as sophisticated as today and even when I started reading the forecasts in 1969 on BBC Radio 2, which then used the long wave frequency, I had to wait for the teleprinter (remember those?) to rattle into life and print out the forecast very noisily, sometimes even standing over it in fear that the roll of paper would run out before the message had finished coming through – aaaarrgh!

Now of course, the broadcast material comes as an attachment to an email – but we all know what can happen to emails and computers, so there are times when I wonder just how much progress has been made in technology. I'm sounding like a Luddite, but only when things go wrong – promise!

And so began the story of how, over the years, this mariners' lifeline has become a cherished institution for listeners on both land and sea. Probably the most listened-to of the four daily Shipping Forecast broadcasts is the one shortly before 1 a.m. It is preceded by its own anthem *Sailing By* (usually only played in part although sometimes there is time to play it in full), written by Ronald Binge. The broadcast version is not available to buy, but there is another version of it available. At the end of a long day, this forecast catches people ready to be lulled into deep somnolence. The slowish pace (unless the forecast is on the long side, most likely in winter when there can be a lot of weather about), the familiarity of the place names, and the sequence of the information (despite its meaning being unclear to the uninitiated), all make for a soothing end to the day – even when the weather itself is rather on the rough side with gales blowing the sailors' socks off!

> *"And finally South East Iceland: cyclonic, becoming north easterly 5 or 6. Occasionally 7. Moderate or good. Rain or showers. Moderate or good. And that ends the shipping bulletin – goodnight!"*
> *(National Anthem – Pips, BBC World Service…)*

And the pattern is the same – night after week after month after year. There is something in many of us that likes the certainties in life and is averse to change. The Shipping Forecast is a comfort, a given, a sign that maybe, just maybe, everything is alright with the world after all – until the next day dawns anyway – but that's a few hours delicious sleep away! Time for the febrile mind to repair itself, rest, chill out, relax and take gentle stock of things.

Over the next few chapters I will expand on the reasons behind the forecast, how it came into being, how it gets on air, how it is received on board ship, and some of the errors that have occurred. There are, not surprisingly, many stories about things that happened when the scripts finally reach the air (see Chapter Eight), which should raise a smile or three. I remember – again when I was working for Radio 2 – that there was a large notice on the wall of the Continuity Studio that read: '*Please engage brain before opening mouth!*' Sounds all too obvious, but there can be many a slip between eye, brain and mouth – oh dear, yes!'

Here as a taster of a forecast that most certainly did NOT get broadcast, but is to be found lurking on the internet. It is read by Brian Perkins and was written by poet Les Barker:

*And now time for the shipping forecast and reports from
    coastal stations.
Here is the general synopsis at 0700 GMT.
Cow in sea area Shannon, moving slowly eastwards and
    filling. Sorry, that should be Low in sea area Shannon.
And now the area reports:
Viking, North Utsire, South Utsire, East Utsire, West Utsire,
    South West Utsire and North North East Utsire:
    wind south west, rain at times, good.
Forties, Fifties, Sixties, Tyne, Dogger, German Bight,*

French Kiss and Swiss Roll: westerly, becoming
   cyclonic, good.
Humber, Thames, Bedford, Leyland-DAF, Dover Sole, Hake,
   Halibut and Monkfish: regular outbreaks of wind,
   rain at times, good.
Wight, Portland, Plymouth, Ginger Rogers and Finisterre:
   light flatulence, some rain, very good.
Lundy, Fundy, Sundy and Mundy: wind south west,
   becoming cyclonic, bloody marvellous.
Rockall: sod all wind, heavy showers, absolutely incredible.
Malin, Hebrides, Bailey, Fair Isle, Cardigan, Pullover and
   South East Iceland: wind south east, rain at times,
   slightly disappointing.
And now the reports for coastal stations:
Tiree: wind north west, 7 miles, one thousand and four,
   rising slowly.
Butt of Lewis: north, 5 miles, one thousand and six, falling.
Wolverhampton: north west, as far as the ring road,
   nine nine eight, rising slowly.
Norway: nil points!

TWO

—

THE GENESIS OF THE
SHIPPING FORECAST

Bear with me for a moment while I explain how inventive man has been on his long journey through evolution. Don't worry, I have taken the liberty of a few shortcuts – the odd million years here or there. When man first crawled out of the primordial slime, he decided to take a shower under a nearby waterfall, then recognised his need for a house, which was cunningly disguised as a cave where he decided to decorate the walls with some hand-drawn pictures, knowing that then – as now – the nearest Ikea was at least a hundred miles and several millennia away. He happened upon a female of the species to share his cave and provide him with some of his manly requirements, leaving him to do the hunting, including of course the filling for those tasty rat pies. Time marched on, progress was made, and then a Roman gentleman named Caesar decided to visit from the continent, risking all against the blue woad-covered locals and Boadicea's lethal hubcaps. These Romans were a clean lot and liked their baths, which got built here and there, although they were not for the plebeian foot soldiers of course, just for the officers and visiting dignitaries – the nobs of the day. They started to build some of the finest roads to speed their progress northwards and soon encountered the Scottish hordes, who would insist on leaving their own land to raid England. The Romans built a wall named after Emperor Hadrian, but still the Scots manage even to this day to infiltrate every corner of the media. The seas were no barrier to invaders from further afield, be they Norse, French or Spanish, and the Brits became quite cunning in their ability to afford the motherland a suitable maritime protection. During all this it became painfully apparent that some form of warning set-up needed to be organised. Not only should there be a good look-out system against any marauding invaders by sea, but it would be advantageous if any adverse weather conditions could be put to good use by the English and be made to work against any invading parties. First of all there were bonfires set on high coastal ground to send warnings along the coast, and they were also lit inland to warn against anything that might be a threat to the sovereign state. These, it must be said, were very effective for several hundred years.

Man's inventiveness continued apace of course, as it always has done and doubtless always will. Now let us leap forward around 1500 years. The Meteorological Office – or Met Office as it is usually called – was first established as the Meteorological Department of the Board of Trade in 1854. Its first boss was Captain (later Vice-Admiral) Robert FitzRoy, who will crop up again later in more detail in Chapter Three. Regular listeners to the Shipping Forecast will recognise his surname as a shipping area, although he is probably best known as the Captain of HMS *Beagle* on its 1831 – 1836 expedition to South America, when he was accompanied by a certain young naturalist named Charles Darwin. It was FitzRoy who introduced the British storm warning service in 1861, but it was not until the 1870s that the electric telegraph enabled far more rapid transmission of information than had hitherto been possible. This – yes, you've guessed it – was when it became possible to develop an observational network throughout the land informing of local weather conditions in order to provide those about to enter or leave our waters, and beyond, with a reasonably up-to-date weather forecast. FitzRoy coined the word 'forecast' himself, and in 1879 the Met Office began supplying an official shipping forecast to the British press. This brings to mind the image of some poor lonely mariner being tossed about on an angry sea while desperately trying to read his rain-sodden *Daily Whatever*, before it once more became unreadable pulp – by which time he would have already known that he was in the proverbial. All this was in the name of safety.

So, this network of observation posts, or stations as they were called, was busy collecting weather data and spreading the word to interested parties about what to expect when they set sail or indeed whether it would be a good idea to set sail at all. Gale warnings were telegraphed to the places most likely to be affected by high winds that day. A new language emerged as the messages were coded with phrases like 'north cone' or 'south cone', meaning northerly or southerly gales. Upon receiving the message, coastguards raised red flags along coasts that were going to be subjected to high winds. During the night, lanterns were used instead; candles were obviously a no-no, as they would have been blown out in a jiffy! When you think about it, it was just a more manageable modern-day version of those bonfires of old – just no more popping back to the nearest village for firelighters. On the next page, you can see some examples of the signals that were used.

Those of you of a certain age will remember that before British Telecom was called BT, the organisation was called the General Post Office or the GPO. As far back as 1911 it was 'broadcasting' gale warnings by telegraph to shipping in the eastern North Atlantic that was heading for the British Isles. The gathering of weather information was by now a two-way exchange from ship to shore, as data gathered from ships in the Atlantic was sent back as advance warning to British shores.

The GPO's telegraphic gale warning service was withdrawn during World War I and not resumed until 1921. Because of the huge help to shipping that this service had provided before the war, it was decided that more support should be given to sailors, and so from 1924 a twice-daily bulletin called *Weather Shipping* was broadcast from the Air Ministry in London, using a very powerful 'continuous wave' (CW) transmitter whose signals could be received up to 2400 miles to the west and about 2000 miles to the south.

We are now nearing the time when the BBC became involved, but not before another form of transmission was tried, called spark transmission. Large ocean-going ships were equipped with the aforementioned CW wireless telegraphy reception but smaller vessels – for cost reasons – were not, and they used this cheaper technology instead. It used a very early type of radio transmitter in which power was generated by discharging a capacitor through an inductor in series with a spark gap – I hope that means more to you than it does to me. However, what was really needed was a single method of transmitting the bulletins that was accessible to everybody who needed it – and this is where the BBC came into the story.

From October 1925, the six-part *Weather Shipping* bulletin – with the exception of Part Two, which was coded – was broadcast twice a day by telephony from the BBC station 5XX at Daventry on 1600 metres long wave. Coverage was extended in 1932 to reach the northern sea areas to aid the increasing number of fishing trawlers in this region. These broadcasts continued until the outbreak of World War II in 1939, and resumed again in 1945 in much the same format.

SMALL CRAFT
SIGNALS

—

DAYTIME SIGNALS (FLAGS)

SMALL CRAFT   GALE   WHOLE GALE   HURRICANE

NIGHT SIGNALS (LIGHTS)

SMALL CRAFT   GALE   WHOLE GALE   HURRICANE

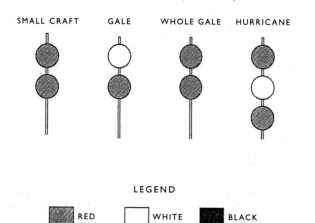

LEGEND

RED   WHITE   BLACK

The inter-war years had also been a time of change for the BBC itself. As mentioned earlier, before the BBC existed, various Government departments had looked after the wireless telegraphy broadcasts. The British Broadcasting Company was formed in 1922 and then became subsumed into The British Broadcasting Corporation in 1927, publicly owned and funded by the Licence Fee Payer – us! We are talking pre-TV days here, so this was just a Radio Licence. Although the BBC was (and is) editorially independent from the government of the day, it was set up to be run very like a government department as this was the 'business model' that seemed to work best at the time – apparently. Some would say that nothing much has changed over the last 80-plus years. It is still run like a government department – although many times bigger than when it began business, and though battles are regularly fought between the government and the Corporation's governing body, it maintains its editorial independence and one hopes always will do.

Regardless of all that, it is the BBC that broadcasts the forecasts. After World War II, they went out on the new Light Programme, restructured in 1967 and renamed BBC Radio 2 broadcasting on long wave. The allocation of wavelengths was altered in November 1978: the final Shipping Forecast on Radio 2 went out on November 22nd, read by Jimmy Kingsbury. The forecasts then switched to Radio 4, which had been moved to long wave in the reallocations. Radio 4 198/200 or 1500 metres long wave has the reach needed to enable the forecasts to be heard for a great distance all round the British Isles, and it has been there ever since.

THREE

—

NAME CHANGING BUT
NOT NAME CALLING

The names of our shipping areas are often accepted without question, just as we accept the naming of so many everyday things and places without really spending too much time in asking 'why'. You probably already have a rough idea of where at least some of the sea areas are – the one that springs to mind is Dover: think Kent coast and you are there! But others are far from obvious and perhaps now is a good time to delve into the whys and wherefores and also what has brought about changes in name or area covered. For some, changing the names of our sea areas causes consternation and a sense of loss, as an old friend vanishes forever.

The most recent one was in 2002, when the late lamented Finisterre off north-western Spain became known as FitzRoy, after a multitude of meetings and the signing of an International Accord between the UK, France, Spain, Portugal and Morocco, who all had to agree on the co-ordination of their shipping area names. Nothing is straightforward in these matters! Finisterre, which derives from the Spanish *finis terre* (the end of the earth – which it probably seemed like to seafarers of old), had to have a new name as the Spanish also use that name for another sea area and they obviously wanted to avoid confusion – fair enough, but what to do? The Met Office delved into its archives and came up with the idea of 'FitzRoy' – why? Well, Vice-Admiral FitzRoy was the first professional weatherman and indeed the founder of the Met Office back in 1854. Good a reason as any! There then followed a ding-dong about how the name should be pronounced. Should it be *FITZ-roy* or *Fitz-ROY*? The former version won. Nothing is ever plain sailing when it comes to the pronunciation of the English language.

Let's look at some historical maps to get an idea of how areas were expanded and how this led to various alterations in naming.

Original shipping areas (1924)

WESTERN AREA

SHETLANDS

HEBRIDES

FORTIES

EASTERN AREA

TAY

CLYDE

HUMBER

DOGGER

SHANNON

MERSEY

THAMES

SEVERN

WIGHT

CHANNEL

SOUTHERN AREA

Shipping areas eight years later in 1932

First we have a diagram showing how the shipping areas were initially defined in 1924 when the *Weather Shipping* broadcasts began. In 1948 the authorities expressed the view that the forecasts should cover a far wider area than before. The seas were once again safe from the prowling wartime U-boats, and the volume of shipping of every kind was increasing exponentially. The following year (see the 1949 chart following) the compass point labels of the general sea areas were dropped and one or two areas were also renamed, resulting in a shipping area map that looks more or less as we see it today.

Shipping areas in 1949

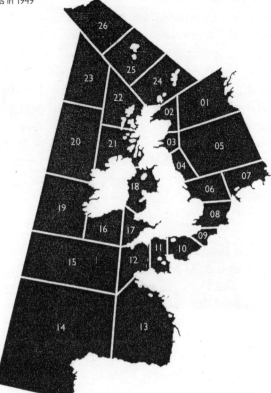

01 FORTIES	10 WIGHT	19 SHANNON
02 CROMARTY	11 PORTLAND	20 ROCKALL
03 FORTH	12 PLYMOUTH	21 MALIN
04 TYNE	13 BISCAY	22 HEBRIDES
05 DOGGER	14 FINISTERRE	23 BAILEY
06 HUMBER	15 SOLE	24 FAIR ISLE
07 HELIGOLAND	16 FASTNET	25 FAEROES
08 THAMES	17 LUNDY	26 ICELAND
09 DOVER	18 IRISH SEA	

In 1955 interested parties from countries bordering the North Sea proposed that wonderfully named Heligoland should assume the same name it was known by on the other side of the North Sea and become German Bight. They didn't stop there, as three other changes were agreed. The first of these was to split Dogger, with the north-eastern half named Fisher. Next on the shopping list, or should that be shipping list, was Forties, which was also split, with the northern half called Viking. Last but not least, the third proposal was that Iceland should become South East Iceland. After no doubt many meetings round tables with fish and chips and glasses of ale, these suggestions were ratified and came into use the following year 1956, as shown on the map below. This is how things remained for almost three decades.

In 1983 the Hebrides sea area to the north west of Scotland was enlarged to include Minches, between the mainland and the Hebrides, and the island of Benbecula. A friend and former colleague Corrie Corfield once had a cat named Benbecula – a splendid name for a feline. The next alteration came in 1984 with the introduction of North and South Utsire. For those of you who like eating herrings, this has some small significance, in that these areas were named after Utsira*, a small island off the west coast of Norway that becomes very popular in the spring when the herring fishing season is at its height. This was agreed on by all the countries bordering the North Sea region. No more changes surely? Well, all remained quiet until the 2002 loss of Finisterre and its replacement with FitzRoy, which I mentioned at the start of the chapter. So let's use this opportunity to take a closer look at the great man, who I hope you will find as interesting as I did.

* The island changed its name from Utsire to Utsira in 1924
but the old spelling is used for the sea area.

SHIPPING AREAS IN USE

BETWEEN 1956 & 1984

—

STATIONS WHOSE LATEST
REPORTS ARE BROADCAST
IN THE 5-MIN FORECASTS

W	WICK
B	BELL ROCK LIGHTHOUSE
D	'DOWSING' LIGHT-VESSEL
G	'GALIOPER' LIGHT-VESSEL

R.S	'ROYAL SOVEREIGN' LIGHT-VESSEL
P.B	PORTLAND BILL
S	SCILLY ISLES
V	VALENTIA
R	RONALDSWAY
P	PRESTWICK
T	TIREE

SHIPPING AREAS

01	VIKING	15	BISCAY
02	FORTIES	16	FINISTERRE
03	CROMARTY	17	SOLE
04	FORTH	18	LUNDY
05	TYNE	19	FASTNET
06	DOGGER	20	IRISH SEA
07	FISHER	21	SHANNON
08	GERMAN BIGHT	22	ROCKALL
09	HUMBER	23	MALIN
10	THAMES	24	HEBRIDES
11	DOVER	25	BAILEY
12	WIGHT	26	FAIR ISLE
13	PORTLAND	27	FAEROES
14	PLYMOUTH	28	S.E. ICELAND
		29	N. ICELAND
		30	DENMARK STRAIT

WEST

NORTHER

SECTION

WEST

CENTRAL

SECTION

WEST

SOUTHER

SECTION

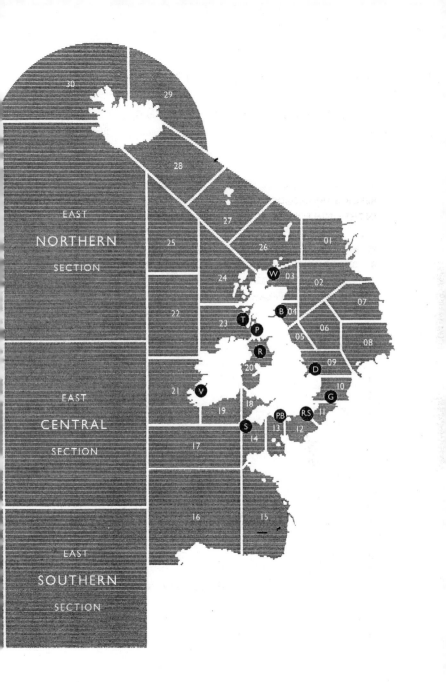

On April 5th, 1805 there was born in Suffolk a Robert FitzRoy and hereby hangs his tale.

Childhood was short in them there days as indeed could be life itself. FitzRoy was trained at the Royal Naval College, which was then a school for cadets, and entered the Navy at the tender age of 14. Over the next decade, he was to see service in the Mediterranean, and in South America, where he was given his first command, that of the good ship *Beagle* in 1828, which was engaged in survey work off the coasts of Patagonia and Tierra del Fuego until 1830.

This experience proved very useful as in 1831 he was once again aboard the *Beagle* commissioned to continue the 1830 survey, this time with Charles Darwin on board – another story for another day. The next few years were spent mainly off South America, initially in the Atlantic Ocean and then in the Pacific Ocean, before heading on to Australia, South Africa and eventually back to England. During the trip FitzRoy ran a chronometric line around the globe, 'forming' – to quote from his report at the time – "*A connected chain of meridian distances around the world, the first that had ever been completed, or even attempted, by means of chronometers alone.*"

In 1835 at the age of 30, he was promoted to Captain. This was a year before he returned to England, where he wrote up his experiences of both those lengthy voyages, which contained a huge amount of information about the physical features of those lands and their peoples.

FitzRoy was by now a very good and experienced surveyor, a point made by Sir Francis Beaufort, Hydrographer to the Navy (I will tell you more about him in Chapter Four), who in a report to the House of Commons extolled the virtues and abilities of

FitzRoy in glowing terms.

In 1841 FitzRoy entered Parliament as member for Durham, and was very active in the House trying to improve the standing of the Mercantile Marine. Two years later he was made Governor of New Zealand, but he proved to be of little success in this post and he was recalled to London shortly afterwards.

He had one more period back at sea commanding the *Arrogant*, an early screw frigate that he had fitted out under his supervision to enable him to carry out more experiments. Once these were completed, he asked to be relieved of his duties on the grounds of ill health, thus ending his very active sea career. Some while later, because of his seniority and experience, he was made first Rear Admiral in 1857, and then Vice-Admiral in 1863.

His work was far from over though. His earlier voyages aboard the *Beagle* had instilled in him a fascination for the weather, supported by his accrued knowledge. This was recognised by the President of the Royal Society, who in 1854 made FitzRoy Meteorological Statistician to the Board of Trade, heading a new department that was later to become the Met Office, and making him responsible for overseeing the collection of weather data at sea. In 1859 there was the mother and father of a storm off the British Isles, which caused the loss of the *Royal Charter*; this led FitzRoy to try visualising weather conditions at any given time by using a synoptic chart from which he could foretell, or as he put it 'forecast' the weather.

He set up a number of telegraph stations to convey weather information back to London to enable a forecast to be made, which was then transmitted to the relevant places where storm warning cones (which we saw in Chapter One) were raised at the ports where gales were expected. Many thousands of seamen over the years had much to thank FitzRoy for in respect of this life-saving gale warning service.

In 1863 he published his *Weather Book*, which was much in advance of scientific thinking of the time. He then went on to spend a great deal of time and energy on improving the work and conditions of the Lifeboat Institutions. Sadly his ferocious hard work throughout his life took its toll. This, coupled with a highly strung disposition and an inability to reconcile his conscience with his religious convictions, led him to commit suicide on April 30th, 1865 at the age of 60.

It must not be forgotten that along with all his industrious work already mentioned, he somehow found time to design and distribute barometers, which also had their place in helping to save lives. So how does a barometer work, I hear you ask? Its purpose is to measure the air pressure and so gauge the probable weather outlook in the coming hours. Let's make it easy and assume you are at sea level – about to set sail or go for a walk with the dog on the beach – the reading at this level is 1013 millibars. The barometer is about a metre high and comprises a glass tube partially filled with mercury, at the base of which there is a reservoir filled with the same matter but open to the air. It's like a pair of scales in a way – balancing outside air pressure against the weight of the column of mercury. The whole apparatus is attached to a piece of wood on which there are measurement markings. In a low-pressure situation, air rises away from the ground more quickly than any surrounding air can fill the gap. The air becomes lighter above the reservoir, the heavier mercury drops in the tube down into the reservoir and when it stops you can read off how low the pressure has become. For higher pressure, the reverse occurs – the reservoir is under greater pressure, so mercury is pushed up the tube until the pressures balance again, giving you a high pressure reading on the barometer mount.

FitzRoy designed two types of barometer: the domestic one, often presented in quite ornate cases popular at the time, and the more robust storm barometer, which was to be found at ports to warn sailors of impending good or bad weather. A few original working examples of FitzRoy barometers still exist, some of which are in the Science Museum in London. Reproductions were made in the 20th century, which are no doubt adorning household walls up and down the land, and may still be being made to this day.

Seldom can a man with such a meteorological pedigree have been more suited to have a sea area named after him and thus have his name immortalised forever. I wonder what this talented man would have thought of having shipping forecasts broadcast four times a day on the radio:

"FitzRoy: north east 5 or 6, occasionally 7, but variable 3 in south. Moderate or rough. Rain or thundery showers, fog patches in south. Moderate or good, occasionally very poor in south"

SO NOW YOU KNOW!

—

As to how the remainder of the shipping areas came to be named, well here's a quick rundown. Some are surprising, others less so perhaps. I'll go into more detail about the history and geography of each area in Chapters Nine and Ten.

The North Sea is littered with sandbanks – and avoiding being caught on these is vital for the safety of shipping. Viking, Forties, Dogger and Fisher are all named after their respective sandbanks. To the west of the Scilly Isles, there is another called Sole and then much further north and to the west between Scotland and Ireland there is Bailey.

Other sea areas are named after islands, including as I mentioned earlier North and South Utsire off the west coast of Norway, but also Wight after the Isle of Wight off the south coast of England, and Lundy visible off the north Devon coast in the Bristol Channel. Fastnet is about six miles to the south of Ireland making it the most southerly point of the Republic of Ireland. Rockall barely qualifies as an island as it is little more than a stack of rocks that poke out through the waves if they are not too high.

Then there are those named after major river estuaries or firths, including Cromarty, Forth, Tyne, Shannon, Humber and Thames. Others are named after geographical regions or places, and these include Dover, Portland, Biscay, Irish Sea, Malin, Hebrides, Fair Isle, Faeroes and of course South East Iceland.

The final two areas are named after bights, the area between the curve of two headlands where the water is shallower than in a bay. The first is, of course, German Bight, named after the area between the Netherlands and Denmark; the other is Trafalgar, off Spain.

Most of the decisions on name and area alterations over the years have been completely outside the control of the Met Office because so many other countries were involved. The march of time and improvements in technology, not to mention the grim reaper otherwise known as cost cutting, have had their effect, such as the automation of light vessels or in some cases their replacement by unmanned buoys. Safety has always remained a priority though and in spite of so much automation, the accuracy of all the data needed has remained paramount. I daresay there will be other upheavals in the future for both good and possibly puzzling reasons.

One such automated light vessel weather station was some years ago parked – sorry, I mean moored – off Norfolk's east coast. It was the *Smith's Knoll Light Vessel*, whose name had a certain mouth-filling satisfaction when I read it out – I don't know why. Its rather more prosaic name was *Trinity House Light Vessel No 72*, which doesn't have quite the same ring about it. (I'll tell you more abut Trinity House in Chapter Eleven.) The vessel was built in 1903 and had a long and busy life: Its claim to fame was that it was commissioned as part of the D-Day Landings, where its task was to mark a safe passage through a German minefield for the landing craft on the way to the Normandy beaches. It was even renamed *Juno* for the task. After the war it had many other postings but was finally decommissioned in 1972 and sold to a company who wanted to scrap her. For whatever reason this didn't happen and the poor old dear is still to be found abandoned and rusting away at a berth near a scrap yard just outside Swansea. Some years ago there was a plan to have her converted into a floating night club, but it came to nothing. I'm sure if this ship had been human she would have felt that this was a bit below her Plimsoll line, so to speak. So there ends the story of but one of these multi-tasking ships that kept other shipping off sandbanks and rocks plus that valiant task in World War II – ending her working life as a Met Office Automatic Weather Station. I salute you, my good old friend *Smith's Knoll Automatic*.

INSHORE WATERS

—

When looking at the geographical location of sea areas, I must also mention the Inshore Waters Forecast, which forms part of the late bulletin just before 0100 and the early bulletin at 0520. This also runs from the north east and goes around the British Isles ending back where it began at Cape Wrath. To remind you of the order it goes like this:

From Cape Wrath to Rattray Head
Rattray Head to Berwick upon Tweed
Berwick upon Tweed to Whitby
Whitby to Gibraltar Point
Gibraltar Point to North Foreland
North Foreland to Selsey Bill
Selsey Bill to Lyme Regis
Lyme Regis to Land's End
Land's End to St David's Head including the Bristol Channel
St David's Head to Great Orme's Head including
    St George's Channel
Great Orme's Head to Mull of Galloway
Lough Foyle to Carlingford Lough
Mull of Galloway to Mull of Kintyre including the Firth
    of Clyde and North Channel
Mull of Kintyre to Ardnamurchan Point
Ardnamurchan Point to Cape Wrath

With the Shetland Isles, Isle of Man and Channel Islands getting a mention, but not all the time.

The map on the following page may make it clearer:

Map showing regions used in the Inshore Waters Forecast.

01 CAPE WRATH – RATTRAY HEAD
    INC. ORKNEY
02 RATTRAY HEAD – BERWICK
03 BERWICK – WHITBY
04 WHITBY – THE WASH
05 THE WASH – NORTH FORELAND
06 NORTH FORELAND – SELSEY BILL
07 SELSY BILL – LYME REGIS
08 LYME REGIS – LANDS END –
    HARTLAND POINT
09 HARTLAND POINT –
    ST DAVID'S HEAD

10 ST DAVID'S HEAD –
    COLWYN BAY
11 COLWYN BAY – MULL OF
    GALLOWAY & ISLE OF MAN
12 MULL OF GALLOWAY – MULL OF
    KINTYRE & NORTH CHANNEL
13 LOUGH FOYLE – CARLINGFORD
    LOUGH
14 MULL OF KINTYRE –
    ARDNAMURCHAN
15 ARDNAMURCHAN – CAPE
    WRATH & THE WESTERN ISLES

FOUR

—

THE METEOROLOGICAL OFFICE AND THE SHIPPING FORECAST BROADCASTS

As already mentioned, what we now call the Met Office, was formed in 1854 when Vice-Admiral Robert FitzRoy was tasked by the Board of Trade with setting up the British Meteorological Department, which he headed for 11 years. He went some way beyond his brief by personally organising for an unofficial daily forecast to be published in *The Times*, although perhaps it didn't enjoy the levels of accuracy possible today. In 1861 he launched a storm warning system, making harbourmasters responsible for raising warning signs to indicate both wind speed and direction.

After his untimely death, the department he had brought into being continued to grow rapidly and began gathering weather data from far and wide, indeed the world over. From 1909 much of the information gathered was transmitted by radio from ship to shore. The next challenge was to cater for the emerging requirements of those amazing men in their flying machines, who needed even more accurate weather information. In 1912 the Meteorological Department inaugurated a weather station in South Farnborough, Hampshire, responsible for providing forecasts to pilots. In 1920, after World War I, the Meteorological Department became part of the Air Ministry, which in turn was part of the Ministry of Defence and based in Adastral House, Kingsway, London. This association was why in those days when listening to the radio you would hear references to the weather as it was on the Air Ministry roof.

Between the wars, the Met Office as it was now known, continued to expand. It used RAF airfields as observation and data-collection points, hence the references to them in weather reports then, and even now for that matter, an example being Leuchars in Fife. In 1936 the Royal Navy parted company with the RAF and decided to provide its own forecasts.

During World War II, the efforts of the Met Office played a part in the D-Day landings. They spotted that a small high-pressure system was going to make a degree of difference to the timing, and it was on the advice of the Met Office that the landings were postponed for 24 hours and so took place on June 6th, 1944 instead of a day earlier. As luck would have it, the German forecasters had not spotted this vital bit of information.

Some years later in 1953, tragic tidal flooding hit the eastern coasts of England, and led the Met Office to introduce the Storm Tide Forecasting Service so as to be able to warn of any future catastrophic tidal incursion on our shores.

The Met Office moved out of London in 1962 to set up a new base in Bracknell, Berkshire in a new purpose-built building, opened by HM The Queen. Computers were used for the first time to aid weather pattern predictions. In 1964 the first satellite pictures of cloud formations were produced. The development of computers now gathered speed and in 1991 the Met Office installed what they called the 'Cray Twins', a pair of supercomputers that were more reliable and accurate than anything used before. Weather patterns and systems are now routinely mapped worldwide, utilising the huge capacity of supercomputers to plot exactly, or at worst roughly, what is going to happen where and when.

The ultra-modern new home of the Met Office in Fitzroy Road, Exeter

The age of both the building and the technology within took its toll on available space and plans were laid for another move in 2003, this time to a brand new complex situated in FitzRoy Road in Exeter, Devon. This was no mean feat as the Met Office had to keep on providing all its worldwide services for the Ministry of Defence and the Civil Aviation Authority without a break.

This new building has two huge supercomputer halls, housing the processing power to do billions of calculations every second. A great deal of the work is covered by the Official Secrets Act, with very specific forecasting carried out for Governments, the military, international companies, airlines and many more organisations all over the world.

Among many other tasks, the collation and writing of the Shipping Forecast takes place within this very building in Exeter. So now let's take a look at the broadcasts themselves.

The Shipping Forecasts are read at 0520, 1201, 1754 and 0048. The last three are read by the duty announcer, but the early morning one is read by the duty weather forecaster from the BBC Weather Centre. These have a summary of gale warnings, the general synopsis and area forecasts for the specified areas around the UK. The early and late forecasts are also followed by a UK Inshore Waters Forecast (as opposed to coastal waters). This covers an area up to 12 miles offshore and for a period up to 1800 the next day. It includes the wind direction and force, visibility and prevailing weather. There is also a rundown of available reports of wind direction and force, visibility, sea level pressure and tendency for about 20 stations around the UK.

The Shipping Forecast always goes out on long wave on all four daily transmissions.

First thing in the morning at 0520 it is on both long wave and FM (Frequency Modulation) in the period leading up to the News Briefing on Radio 4. The reason for this being that there is no call for any other information to go out separately on FM at this time of day, plus of course the increased costs of so doing in any case. The same reasoning applies to the late night forecast at 0048 when the forecast goes out on both frequencies preceded by *Sailing By*. Although the sound quality on FM is a good deal clearer, the broadcast range of the FM transmitters is far more restricted by the nature of frequency modulation over long wave, plus there are restrictions on the amount of power that an individual transmitter is allowed to use, to prevent it causing interference to another station using the same frequency. These restrictions were introduced when local radio came on the scene – demand for more frequencies from the very restricted frequency allocation that had formerly been available was solved by the sharing of frequencies on reduced power. There was also a huge upheaval in who used which frequencies under the Geneva Frequency Plan in 1975 when many low frequency (LF) and medium frequency (MF) broadcast stations across Europe were changed. The result is that FM can only be heard up to about 10 or 12 miles offshore at best, so its use is strictly limited to shipping close to land, be it large or small.

Radio 4 splits its transmissions at 1200, to allow for a four-minute news bulletin to go out on FM only, while on long wave there is a one-minute news summary followed by the three-minute forecast. The two frequencies come together again at 1204 for *You & Yours*.

At 1754 there is once again a split in programming towards the end of *PM* which remains on Radio 4 FM, while on long wave there is the forecast followed by a brief national conventional weather forecast for those of us on dry land followed by (if time) a brief programme run down for the evening ahead on Radio 4. Then both networks join together again in time for the chimes of Big Ben and the 1800 news.

There is a departure from this at weekends in as far as the 1201 and the 1754 forecasts go out on both Radio 4 frequencies as it is easier and cheaper to schedule them that way. Nothing more complex than that. This is mainly due to the different programming on these two days at these times which just makes it simpler to do things this way.

So within this rigid schedule, the Forecast must get across all the information that users need to know. However, the state of the weather around our shores varies, of course, depending as much as anything on the time of year. More detail is required, to put it simply, in the winter months when there are a large number of weather systems battering our shores from different directions and with varying amounts of ferocity than on a lovely summer's day in June where we are in the middle of a slow-moving or stationary warm system sucking up warm air from North Africa or the Gulf Stream. That said, the number of words the forecast may contain is strictly limited by the BBC to 350 as – regardless of what the weather is doing – the airtime for that forecast remains the same. This can pose quite a challenge to the forecast compiler down in Exeter!

There is a bit more flexibility in the late forecast at 0048, when there is not only the Shipping Forecast but also the Inshore Waters Forecast, plus a short UK outlook if there is time. The actual time slot for this particular bulletin is 11 minutes, which means that sometimes it is a bit of a squeeze to get it all in while at other times it is quite comfortable from the point of view of the person reading it. If the Forecast overruns, the hand-over from Radio 4 to the BBC World Service (which broadcasts on the Radio 4 frequencies from 0100 until 0520) can be delayed by one minute, by missing the Pips and the 0100 news headlines, and then joining cleanly for the news itself at one minute past one, but this is rarely necessary.

An 11-minute read is quite demanding, knowing that you have a good deal of information to impart and that the listening conditions for your primary audience are not always, shall we say, ideal. Many professional users of the forecast will record it and then listen back to the part of the information that most affects them. Then of course there are other audiences, those who just like to listen to this unique piece of prose before they drop off to sleep. They are listening in perfect conditions propped up in bed safely away from the rigours of the British weather, enjoying the delivery of these familiar names and places and maybe feeling quietly smug that they are out of harm's way or not really noticing or even caring that much about the content – just listening to a warm familiar voice lulling them off to sleep.

"And finally the UK Outlook for the next 24 hours:

High pressure over southern England will weaken, allowing low pressure systems to the north of Scotland and in the North Atlantic to dominate the weather across the UK. This will bring strong to gale force winds to much of the country. And that ends this shipping bulletin."

At the risk of getting bogged down with detail, perhaps this is a good place to explain what all the terms and descriptive words mean in the forecasts.

The forecasts always begin with a gale warning (if there is one). If there are many gales blowing leaving only four or fewer areas without them, then the wording is "There are warnings of gales in all areas except x, y and z". This helps keep the word count down.

The word *then* takes on some importance as if an area has two types of weather it is the most severe one that takes precedence – for example *rain then showers*.

The next word to explain is *occasional*, which relates to a weather type appearing more than once for less than half of the forecast period. For instance, *occasionally poor* or *occasional rain*.

For a time or *at times* is something which happens once for no more than half the forecast period.

At first refers to an occurrence at the start of the forecast period but ceasing by the middle.

Later means starting more than half way through the period and continuing to the end but the weather writer's style guide prefers the use of the word *becoming* i.e. *rain at first becoming fair*.

Soon is weather expected within six to twelve hours of the forecast time of issue.

Imminent is weather expected within six hours of time of issue.

Perhaps as the word suggests describes some uncertainty of what will happen in the forecast period.

Wind direction terms are north, south, north west, south west, etc. and up to two directions are allowed for instance *south or south west*. If the wind moves out of the designated range, then the words *backing* or *veering* are used. If the wind alters in both speed and direction then the direction takes precedence: *south veering south west, 4 increasing 5 or 6*.

Now as far as gale warnings are concerned, they are measured on the Beaufort Scale (more about Sir Francis Beaufort at the end of this chapter).

I love the word *precipitation*, which means that something is falling from the heavens to land on our heads be it snow (*solid precipitation*) or rain (*liquid precipitation*). Then there are *showers*, which can be one or the other.

Just one more category to baffle you with and that is the movement of pressure systems on the following page.

GALE FORCE 8

34–40 KNOTS WITH GUSTS
REACHING 43–51 KNOTS

SEVERE GALE FORCE 9

41–47 KNOTS REACHING GUSTS
OF 52–60 KNOTS

STORM FORCE 10

48–55 KNOTS REACHING GUSTS
OF 61–68 KNOTS

VIOLENT STORM FORCE 11

56–63 REACHING GUSTS OF
69 KNOTS OR MORE

HURRICANE FORCE 12

64 KNOTS OR MORE

—

HURRICANE FORCE 12 IS NOT TO BE
VENTURED OUT INTO IF AT ALL POSSIBLE
FOR VERY OBVIOUS REASONS. THE USE
OF HURRICANE FORCE IS TO DISTINGUISH IT
FROM THE WORD HURRICANE, WHICH ON
ITS OWN MEANS A TROPICAL CYCLONE, WHICH
IS, OF COURSE, NOT EXPERIENCED IN
OUR NORTHERLY CLIMES

Now we come to terms that describe visibility:

GOOD

IS VISIBILITY FOR MORE THAN
5 NAUTICAL MILES

MODERATE

BETWEEN 2 AND 5 NAUTICAL MILES

POOR

BETWEEN 1000 METRES AND
2 NAUTICAL MILES

FOG

LESS THAN 1000 METRES

FOG PATCHES

COVER LESS THAN 40%
OF THAT SEA AREA

FOG BANKS

COVER 40–50% OF
THAT SEA AREA

EXTENSIVE FOG

COVER MORE THAN 50%
OF THAT SEA AREA

Now, if you are so inclined, you can understand more about that forecast you are listening to and how the writer is, in his few precious, permitted words, distilling this graphic word picture of the prevailing weather around our shores.

THE FORECAST WRITER'S STYLE GUIDE

—

As I explained earlier in this chapter, the timing constraints of the broadcast schedule mean that the BBC asks the Met Office to restrict the maximum number of words for the forecast to 350, with a minimum of not much less than this because if too few words were written, the forecast would have to be read a tad too slowly for comfort, and would sound odd. This imposed word limit is quite testing for both the experienced and new writer of the forecast and on occasion the reader too. There has to be a little bit of leeway, as the list of gale warnings can vary from none to several, and the

SLOWLY

MOVING AT LESS THAN
15 KNOTS

STEADILY

15 TO 25 KNOTS

RATHER QUICKLY

25 TO 35 KNOTS

RAPIDLY

35 TO 45 KNOTS

VERY RAPIDLY

MORE THAN 45 KNOTS

length of the general synopsis can also vary from day to day. But it does take the art of précis writing to new heights.

The format is always the same, starting with the words "And now the Shipping Forecast..." followed by the date and time of issue. Then gale warnings, if there are any, moving next to the general synopsis, followed by the area forecasts for the following 24 hours. The 30 areas always appear in the same order, starting with Viking and ending with South East Iceland. There is one exception to this, in that area Trafalgar, (number 31) only appears in the late night forecast.

The writer's bugbear of limited word numbers concentrates the mind. Words can be saved by grouping as many sea areas together as possible so long as no vital information is lost. Often in groupings it is possible to say something on the lines of "Humber, Thames, Dover, Wight, Portland, Plymouth: moderate, with fog patches becoming good except in Humber and Thames" to show that there is a bit of difference but maintaining clarity and economy of words. The norm is that groupings should be governed by common wind conditions.

The actual content of each area forecast is unchanging and will include: wind, sea state, weather and visibility, plus if appropriate references to icing (which is of serious note for aviation in particular). In describing wind force severity, the word force is always left out with the exception of Hurricane Force 12, as mentioned earlier, to distinguish it from a tropical cyclone. Also in gale warnings a suffix is always used so that the direction is for instance *westerly*.

All forecasts are issued in local time, so it's GMT in winter and BST in summer. So, as you can see, the forecast writer has plenty to think about as he or she sets about compiling each of the four forecasts a day. Sometimes, depending on the stability of the weather, these forecasts are written quite close to the broadcast wire, leaving the reader very little time to prepare. Mostly though, they are written some way ahead.

The difference between *backing* and *veering* is as follows:

If the wind is described as *veering*, it is changing direction in a clockwise direction – so for instance moving from south westerly to west.

If it is *backing*, then it's doing the opposite and going anticlockwise, moving from south east to north east for example.

Wind speed is measured on the Beaufort Wind Scale Chart, which is given in full on p.60, but to break it down to its simplest form it is as follows (See over):

As promised, let's now take a look at the man who invented this scale – Sir Francis Beaufort.

Francis Beaufort was born near Navan in County Meath in Ireland in 1774. His father, a rector, was a respected authority on geography and topography. Like FitzRoy, he joined the Royal Navy very young (aged 13) as a midshipman and pursued an illustrious naval career, serving in the Napoleonic Wars. In 1800, at the age of 26, he received 19 wounds in a battle near Malaga. This did earn him promotion to Commander, but one bullet remained in a lung for the remainder of his life, causing him considerable pain from time to time. If that was not enough, he was wounded again in a battle with pirates off the Turkish coast in 1812. Beaufort was struck in the groin by a shot fired by the pirates, and his hip was fractured. Although he managed to convalesce on board, by the winter his ship was no longer seaworthy and he was ordered home.

It was while in command from 1805 of the *Woolwich*, a 44-gun man-

0

CALM, WITH A FLAT SEA

1

LIGHT AIR, WITH RIPPLES
WITHOUT CRESTS

2

LIGHT BREEZE, WITH SMALL
WAVELETS NOT BREAKING

3

GENTLE BREEZE, WITH LARGE
WAVELETS STARTING TO
BREAK WITH SCATTERED
WHITE CAPS

4

MODERATE BREEZE, WITH SMALL
WAVES WITH BREAKING
CRESTS AND A FEW WHITE HORSES

o-war, that he devised his Wind Force Scale. However, it is worth noting that Beaufort was not the originator of such a scale as one was in use about a century earlier. Before that it is also pretty certain that medieval Arab seafarers used some such scale in the 15th century. Sadly there is a lack of definitive documentation to support any of these claims, so it has to remain educated speculation. The Navy adopted Beaufort's Wind Force Scale in 1838 and, although modified hugely over the next hundred or so years (more on this below), in essence this scale had the 12 variations, from 0 for calm through to 12 for a full Hurricane force, that we are still familiar with today.

At the age of 55, he was appointed Hydrographer to the Royal Navy, a post he held until he was 81. During his time in office he commissioned voyages to survey and chart many areas of the globe. His tireless politicking and wheedling for funds paved the way for many of the great seaborne scientific expeditions in the 19th century, and it was in fact very much down to him that Darwin was able to set sail with FitzRoy onboard the *Beagle* in 1831. Beaufort and FitzRoy were close friends for many years.

Beaufort was an assiduous diarist, and logged his calculations meticulously. However, he kept a second set of diaries, written in a personal cipher. When these were discovered after his death, it was found that he had written of intense emotional and family problems. It is clear that after the death in 1834 of Alicia, his wife of 21 years who had borne him seven children, he began, on a regular basis over a period of three years, an incestuous relationship with his sister Harriet, who kept house for him. They had been very close throughout their lives, and it is thought their relationship intensified between the death of Alicia, and his second marriage in 1838, to Honora Edgeworth.

SPECIFICATIONS AND

BEAUFORT WIND SCALE	MEAN WIND SPEED		LIMITS OF WIND SPEED		WIND DESCRIPTIVE TERMS
	KNOTS	M/S	KNOTS	M/S	
0	0	0	<1	0–0.2	Calm
1	2	0.8	1–3	0.3–1.5	Light air
2	5	2.4	4–6	1.6–3.3	Light breeze
3	9	4.3	7–10	3.4–5.4	Gentle breeze
4	13	6.7	11–16	5.5–7.9	Moderate breeze
5	19	9.3	17–21	8.0–10.7	Fresh breeze
6	24	12.3	22–27	10.8–13.8	Strong breeze
7	30	15.5	28–33	13.9–17.1	Near gale
8	37	18.9	34–40	17.2–20.7	Gale
9	44	22.6	41–47	20.8–24.4	Severe gale
10	52	26.4	48–55	24.5–28.4	Storm
11	60	30.5	56–63	28.5–32.6	Violent storm
12	–	–	64+	32.7+	Hurricane

The Beaufort Wind Scale Chart

EQUIVALENT SPEEDS

PROBABLE WAVE HEIGHT IN METRES	PROBABLE MAX WAVE HEIGHT IN METRES	SEA STATE	SEA DESCRIPTIVE TERMS
–	–	0	Calm (Glassy)
0.1	0.1	1	Calm (Rippled)
0.2	0.3	2	Smooth (Wavelets)
0.6	1.0	3	Slight
1.0	1.5	3 – 4	Slight – Moderate
2.0	2.5	4	Moderate
3.0	4.0	5	Rough
4.0	5.5	5 – 6	Rough – Very rough
5.5	7.5	6 – 7	Very rough – High
7.0	10.0	7	High
9.0	12.5	8	Very high
11.5	16.0	8	Very high
14+	–	9	Phenomenal

He was made Rear-Admiral on the retired list of 1846, knighted two years later, remained as Hydrographer until 1855 and died in 1857. As well as his name living on in the Beaufort Scale, the sea north of Alaska is named after him too.

As mentioned earlier, over the years the Scale has needed modification as ships began to rely less on sail, and instruments became better at measuring the swell and strength of the waves. In 1874 it was altered to reflect the changes in the way warships were rigged, and it was then expanded a couple of decades later to include the sail required by fishing smacks. By the early 20th century, the ending of the use of sail made a specification based on the canvas carried by a sailing ship impractical. The British meteorologist George Simpson proposed an alternative, although this was not adopted by the International Meteorological Organization until 1939.

The extension of the scale to 17 values was undertaken by the International Meteorological Committee in 1946, further defining the strength of hurricane force winds at the top end of the scale, so the ranges of wind speed as measured at a height of 10 metres above the surface were now represented by each Force Number. In effect, the measurements were now of wind speed and wave size, so the Beaufort Wind Force Scale technically became the Beaufort Wind Speed Scale.

The Scale assumed its present form around 1960, with the addition of probable wave heights and probable maximum wave heights.

Rear-Admiral Sir Francis Beaufort 1774 – 1857

FIVE

—

THE LIGHTER SIDE

Rather than risk getting bogged down further in the technicalities of the background to the Shipping Forecast, let's take a break now – with or without a mug of cocoa – and look at how the forecast has caught the imagination of writers and musicians as well as everyday listeners, entrepreneurs and many others who have been inspired to take their slant on this very British institution. The extent of these various reactions is wide-ranging, from quite serious and moving poetry to pop songs, comedy sketches, newspaper articles, and entire books. Indeed, quotes pop up out of our radio and TV sets, on stage and in film.

Being an island race influences the way we feel. We know an unimaginable mighty force of nature surrounds us, manifested in the state of the seas. We can't help being aware in the backs of our minds, if not actually feeling threatened, that on and off shore there is a relentless power, which has also protected us over the centuries from the ravages of marauding hordes. Had we been part of continental Europe, our history would have been very different.

I'm no psychologist, but perhaps when we are listening to that forecast safely tucked up in bed, it is reassuring to know what is happening out there, as we listen and our minds marshal the excesses of the weather into understandable and comforting bite-sized paragraphs of information that in all honesty sanitise, for those of us who don't venture on the open seas, this awesome raw power that man has absolutely no control over whatsoever. It is a comfort for those of us on dry land to know that those at sea have the benefit of the information they so badly need (and understand) so they can believe themselves more in control of their water-borne destiny, allowing us to sleep easy in this knowledge and revel in our dreams with a clear conscience.

So, how exactly has the Forecast influenced our culture and at this point our 'popular' culture? The way it is written and read, plus the familiar and evocative names, give it its own inbuilt poetry. This has attracted song writers and poets to throw in their caps, to weave in their own particular strands to the rich tapestry that is the Shipping Forecast.

Here first of all is an example from the pop group Blur's album *Park Life* with the lyric from a track entitled *This is a Low*:

> *And into the sea goes pretty England and me*
> *Around the Bay of Biscay and back for tea*
> *Hit traffic on the Dogger Bank, up the Thames to find a taxi rank*
> *Sail on by with the tide and go to sleep and the radio says*
> *This is a low but it won't hurt you*
> *When you're alone it will be there with you*
> *Finding ways to stay solo*
> *On the Tyne Forth and Cromarty*
> *There's a low in the high forties*
> *Saturday's locked away on the pier*
> *Not fast enough dear...*

It goes on, but you get the picture. Radiohead were another group whose descriptive juices were sort of inspired by this subject in a song called *In Limbo* – sorry, I have descended into sarcasm here, but you'll understand why as the song appears to go on like this for quite a while:

> *Lundy, Fastnet, Irish Sea*
> *I got a message I can't read*
> *I got a message I can't read...*

Well, at least three areas got a mention but there the needle seemed to stick.

Inspiration seems to have caught on in the pop world with a number of other groups and soloists playing with the forecast to suit their own ends. These include The Young Punx, Tears for Fears, Chumbawamba, Manfred Mann, Jethro Tull and iLIKETRAINS. I had to mention this last one as they asked me to record a bit of a forecast in 2007 over a track (yes, pun intended) they had done, which I recorded in a studio built under the railway arches in Putney in south London. This took rather longer than planned as we had to stop recording every time a train went overhead, be it tube or British Rail, as the rumble of rolling stock was much louder than me. It was one of those times when I had a strange mixture of feelings – ranging from annoyance to amusement – at our attempts at recording something in such a bonkers location. However you wouldn't know by the result – after a fair bit of editing, it could have been the Abbey Road Studios in St John's Wood for all anyone would have known. So the diverse appeal of the forecast begins to assert itself and shows just how many people in so many different walks of life are not only aware of it but actively respond to aspects of its use of language and its poetry, which probably don't chime with other people at all. The human ear is a very selective mechanism, as is the brain it feeds.

Of course there are other random references playing ducks and drakes with the area names, but they are quite fun like a Shakespearian one where someone says they studied *Much Ado About Rockall*, *The Cromarty of Errors* and *Pericles, Prince of Tyne*, followed by *All's Wight that ends Wight* and *Henry the Forth, Parts 1 and 2*.

There is also a reference in the film *Kes* (based on the novel *A Kestrel for a Knave* by Barry Hines), where the school teacher is taking the daily register and calls out "Fisher" whereupon Billy responds "German Bight". Once you start looking, there are so many little references like this, which are both fun and completely harmless.

On a more serious and indeed tender note the poet and broadcaster Sean Street wrote *Shipping Forecast, The Fisherman* and *His Wife in Donegal*:

They have shared still late October,
but salt stones and a broken tree,
the peeled paint on the lifeboat house
chime with places where the glass falls,
prime sources encountering night's bald predictions.

Everywhere winter edges in,
and now the time is ten to six...

Lightness and weight, air's potentials
pressed into words, implication;
here – on all coasts – listening grows passionately tense.

'Fair Isle, Faeroes, South East Iceland,

North Utsire, South Utsire,
Fisher, German Bight, Tyne, Dogger...'
This pattern of names on the sea –
Weather's unlistening geography – paves water.
Beyond the music, the singing
of sounds – this minimal chanting,
this ritual paired to the bones
becomes the cold poetry of information.

The litany edges closer
'Lundy, Fastnet and Irish Sea...'
Routine enough, all just routine,
Always his eyes guessing beyond
the headland, she perhaps sleeping, no words spoken.

He stretches forward to grasp it,
Claims his radio place – 'and now
the weather reports from coastal stations' and then:
    'Malin Head' – such routine that she barely glances
    up, but hears 'now falling'.

The Irish poet Seamus Heaney wrote a sonnet entitled *The Shipping Forecast*, which begins:

Dogger, Rockall, Malin, Irish Sea:
Green, swift upsurges, North Atlantic flux
Conjured by that strong gale-warming voice,
Collapse into a sibilant penumbra.

The Poet Laureate Carol Ann Duffy wrote *Prayer*, which ends with the lines:

Darkness outside. Inside, the radio's prayer – Rockall.
    Malin. Dogger. Finisterre.

It's rather wonderful to think of the forecast being similar to prayer. Then there is this slightly raunchy rendering by Julia Darling entitled *Forecasting*:

He was a viking in his forties.
Tyne after tyne I said, don't dogger me,
just don't dogger me – but he fishered,
me a single parent with no german bite.

I came to like his humber,
and eventually thames towards him.
Dover and dover
we caught the white of each other's lundy,
throwing all faeroes into the fast net,
deep in our Irish sea,
rockallin' and dancin' the malin.
Those were the Hebrides years.
Until Cromarty.

How I wish Cromarty had not met my viking.
Still only forty, we tyned and doggered,
until my fisher ran out.
And he got his german bite all right,
humbering half way up the Thames,
waves dover him,
his white in the dark lundy,
faeroes swept from the fast net.
I have drunk the Irish Sea,
hearing him, calling through ships,
Rockall – Malin – CROMARTY

Thanks Cromarty. I hope you sink,
someday.

Then I found tucked away on a website called poemsgalore, a poem by Kathleen Thorpe who has obviously always been fascinated by place names, not least the sea areas round our coasts. She was inspired to write this poem using some of them – it's called *Moderate Visibility*:

When I was a child long ago,
listening to the radio
with my grandma, sipping tea,
tuning in to the BBC
for the Shipping Forecast every day,
taking in each word they'd say.

Dogger, Fisher, German Bight;
precipitation within sight
away from land and out to sea
with moderate visibility.
Force four south, veering south west later,
warm winds coming from the Equator.
Bailey, Malin Hebrides;
fog clearing in the gentle breeze.
Winds freshen in Finisterre
Blowing rain clouds here and there.
Dover, Wight and Portland Bill,
gale force winds are raging still.
Lundy, Fastnet, Irish Sea
have moderate visibility.
Heavy rain in Tyne and Forth
and a good force nine is moving north
to Cromarty where waves are high,

almost reaching for the sky.
While down in Plymouth the seas are calm,
the forecast says its turning warm,
over a thousand millibars
in clearing skies you'll see the stars.
Grandma, peering over her tea
says 'moderate visibility'.

The former National Poet of Wales, Gillian Clarke, has also written about the forecast in *Farewell Finisterre*:

One a.m., and I'm alone
with the late night announcer.
We navigate the small hours
over Viking, the Utsires, his voice
telling the island's rosary,
the stations of the night.

In the house the bottles are empty,
candles snuffed in their lighthouses,
a pulse of flame before dark fell
on the waters of Dogger, German Bight.
His words home along the airwaves.
Humber, he says, Thames, Dover, Wight.

Windows are doused one by one.
The house sleeps beyond Trafalgar, Finisterre.
The wind picks up and my heart's listening
for Lundy, Irish Sea, till words turn north,
his voice saying Shannon, Rockall,
the far away poetry of Hebrides,

and we wing out over the sea where once

from a plane travelling a latitude beyond
Fairisle, Faeroes, South East Iceland,
I saw far below the coldest word
in the school atlas. Its arctic radio name.
Its plates of ice. Its silence.

Quite a contrast of poetic treatment on a subject that many regard as poetry in its own right. Seeing how radio is the Forecast's home medium, what gems have appeared there over the decades?

Stephen Fry had a crack at the forecast some years ago in his Radio 4 programme *Saturday Night Fry*, which went something like this:

And now before the news and weather, here is the Shipping
Forecast issued by the Met Office at 1400 GMT.
Finisterre, Dogger, Rockall, Bailey: No.
Wednesday, variable, imminent, super.
South Utsire, North Utsire, Sheerness, Foulness, Elliot Ness:
If you will, often, eminent, 447, 22 yards, touchdown, stupidly.

Lots of people have asked if I will be mentioning *The Shipping News*. Well no, not really (even though I just have) as it is a book by Annie Proulx from which a recent film was made set in Newfoundland, yes with a fabulous cast but nothing to do with our coastal waters and way outside this remit. This reminds me though of a few incidences of being told I had been heard doing the 'Shipping Show' – umm, well almost.

The wonderful thing is with all these treatments by writers is that there is no malice, just the mild sending up of something that appeals to so many of us even if there is a partial – or complete – lack of understanding of what it is all about. It has just suffused itself into our written and spoken language, and will probably remain there far into the future. I wonder what my very young grandsons will make of it when they are a bit older. (I know who their parents will point them towards if there are any questions.)

Nowadays, there are all sorts of oddities on the internet relating to the forecast too. One of them is a 'cod' piece that suggests that some years ago there was something of a rift between North and South Utsire that could have put into peril the very existence of the forecast! It 'reports' that no less an august organisation than the UN was prevailed upon by the combined forces of the Met Office, the Maritime and Coastguard Agency (MCA) and BBC Radio 4 to step in and sort things out.

It all began, so they would have us believe, when the Cod War came to an end in 1976. This dispute, you may remember, was between the UK and Iceland over fishing rights in the sea areas to the north west of the British Isles. It even got to the point where the Icelanders employed their gunboats against British shipping trawlers and created something of an international incident, which was thankfully sorted out over a table in the end rather than all-out confrontation on the high seas. That part is of course true. What follows is not, but it is amusing.

Three decades after these events, and after the Utsirers had split from each other, a sort of peace had been maintained by coalition troops from the nearby areas of Viking, Forties and Fisher. That is until a spate of allegations from both sides concerning perceived misdemeanours brought things to a head again. The story goes that North Utsire accused the South of amassing a Gale Force that was *veering northerly, backing southerly*. This was denied of course with the repost from the South that it was merely *moderate or good – mainly fair*. More insults were hurled between the two causing the Commander of the Coalition Force – General Synopsis – to describe the outlook for a return to peace in the area as *slight, occasionally poor, becoming very poor later*.

There then followed reports from neighbouring areas that a rather alarming flow of Utsirian refugees were crossing their borders to escape to safety in the event that things turned really nasty.

Clearly it was time to take this even more seriously. UNHCR began to erect refugee camps in Cromarty, Dogger and German Bight as the flow of Utserian 'boat people' (known as 'trawler men' to the locals) was expected to reach huge numbers.

It was now obvious that all this trouble and hardship was going to have serious ramifications for the Shipping Forecast itself. The then Controller of Radio 4, Mark Damazer, explained the situation saying:

> *"If this escalates into full and open conflict between North and South Utsire, then we will run the very real risk of there being further fragmentation in the region."*

He went on to say:

> *"It takes us long enough to make up the cryptic bollocks for the 30-odd areas that already exist. If we were to add more, there would simply not be enough time to broadcast the forecast."*

He concluded with the following salient words, which it had to be said raised a few thousand eyebrows:

> *"It's the very same reason we have consistently refused forecast membership to the areas Flip-Flop, Italian's Crotch and Cockall!"*

Luckily good sense prevailed, and there is peace once more, albeit an uneasy one if the above were in any way to be believed.

As a footnote to the actuality of the Cod War, I remember falling about one morning during the nine o'clock news bulletin when the reader, a colleague of mine, referred to 'Icelandic gumboots' instead of gunboats.

SIX

—

UNEXPECTED OUTSIDE
BROADCAST

I imagine that you presume the Forecast is broadcast from a studio somewhere deep inside Broadcasting House – and you are absolutely right. Indeed I have never read it from anywhere else. The Radio 4 studios, and for that matter most of the other studios too, are situated in the middle of the building, so that they are shielded from the never-ending mighty roar of London's traffic as it storms up and down Portland Place outside. It's a shame that though they are soundproof (in theory at least), structure-borne sound from within the building itself still seems to leak into the studios from time to time. Drills are a prime example, and the steel girders that form the framework of the building unfortunately act as rather splendid sounding boards, but these things are sometimes unavoidable – when things break, they need to be mended.

What follows now is an unusual, nay unique, account of how my friend and ex-colleague Zeb Soanes found himself reading the Shipping Forecast from very odd – although at the same time somewhat apt – surroundings.

"One day in the spring of 2010 I had a chance to read the Forecast looking out from the Orford Ness lighthouse across the North Sea.

"The Forecast boasts a list of 31 maritime locations, names that evoke a wild seascape of the imagination: Dogger, FitzRoy, Hebrides, Rockall, German Bight... and it's a daily rhythmic recitation that much of the country finds quaintly comforting. Tucked up in bed, the landlubber experiences all the vicarious danger of gales that are *imminent*, and is reassured when conditions are *moderate or good*. This nightly litany of the sea reminds the British that theirs is an island nation with a proud seafaring past.

"For me, it evokes thoughts of home and family. I grew up by the sea in Suffolk on England's east coast. The stretch of coastline running down from my hometown of Lowestoft is heavy with history and with myth. It is also being steadily eaten away by the encroaching waves. Over the years, whole villages have been lost to the sea. Legend has it that on stormy nights, you can still hear the church bells of Dunwich tolling far beneath the waves.

"Now it is the famous lighthouse at Orford Ness in Suffolk that is under threat. The Ministry of Defence commandeered this area and used it for more than 70 years to carry out secret military tests. Work was done here to develop the atomic bomb and perfect the system that later became known as radar. One of the buildings is now used to beam the BBC World Service across the North Sea to western Europe and beyond.

"There are numerous, possibly apocryphal stories about this remote spit of land, which was strictly closed to the general public for many decades. Some believe the tall networks of aerials were first erected to monitor the movement of UFOs. Certainly it's true that one of the benefits of having been a closed military site is that the wildlife was left to flourish, including several rare species that, seemingly, were undisturbed by the frequent explosions and other mysterious military activity.

"The BBC agreed that on this one occasion the Shipping Forecast could be read from the top of the Orford Ness lighthouse, and I met lighthouse keeper Keith Seaman – an appropriately nautical name – over tea in a former Ministry of Defence hut. It turned out that he came from a long line of keepers.

"Keith drove us out across the shingle, past ominous warnings of unexploded bombs – they still find up to 15 a year – to reach the lighthouse. It is mainly white but with two red candy stripes. Keith told me the two stripes are an identification signal to sailors by day, as useful as the light is itself by night. *There's another red and white lighthouse up the coast at Happisburgh, but that has three stripes*, he informed me. The dangers to shipping here have long been notorious. In 1627, 32 ships were lost in a single night here. There was scarcely a survivor.

"This lighthouse stands only metres from the shoreline. It seems poignant and perhaps fitting that a landmark that has stood for 200 years and survived storms, flying bombs and machine-gun fire, may ultimately be swallowed by the sea. Like all modern lighthouses, it is battery-powered, charged by the mains to ensure continuity of service in the event of a power cut. Halfway up, I was surprised to see a computer-station linked to a transmitter on the roof. Therein may lie the fate of all British lighthouses – high-tech navigation systems may soon render them all redundant. But, as Keith noted dryly, *That's all right so long as the computers work.*

"We climbed to the top, and had a wonderful view as it was a beautiful spring day. On a clear night, I was told, the light itself can be seen for 25 nautical miles (46 km). It has a four-tonne lens that floats on a bath of mercury. Keith switched off the motor and showed me how, with a mere touch of my finger, I could start it revolving again.

"And so, finally, I unfolded a copy of that morning's Shipping Forecast, faced out to sea, and started to read. At the BBC headquarters back in London, we broadcast from a windowless studio, so it was a real treat to be able to gaze out and read to the distant crews in boats on the horizons who, as opposed to the landlubbers who simply enjoy its poetry, depend on the Forecast's maritime data to keep them safe.

"The area forecasts for the next 24 hours", I intoned. "German Bight, Humber, Thames. North west backing south west four or five, decreasing three at times. Slight or moderate. Occasional rain. Fog patches. Good, occasionally very poor."

"Of course it all made perfect sense to Keith, the lighthouse keeper, who passed on one final piece of advice to protect those out at sea: My grandfather always said, *'Before you leave, sweep your eyes over the horizon'*. And so before we left, we did."

I suspect that experience was almost certainly a one-off but it adds a certain something to this tale about the Shipping Forecast and how odd stories about it can pop up from all sorts of unexpected places and at the same time add a certain piquancy to the whole.

Just before we move on, Zeb mentioned that the Ministry of Defence (MOD) commandeered this area some time back, and there are still ageing signs to be seen such as *Warning: MOD Property. Keep Out* and *This is a prohibited place within the meaning of the Official Secrets Act. Unauthorised persons entering this area may be arrested and prosecuted*. A salutary warning indeed. There are stories still circulating among a few ufologists in the area that here on what was called the Cobra Mist site there are stored the remains of a spaceship. You pays your money and takes your choice. Cobra Mist was a sophisticated radar system – *over the horizon* as it was called – which was used to keep an eye on Soviet and Chinese activities in the Sixties and early Seventies. The site was not ideal for the intended purpose and was decommissioned in 1973.

SEVEN

—

SAILING BY

"Just before the shipping bulletin, here's part of Sailing By…"

If you are a regular listener to the final forecast of the day, just before one o'clock in the morning, you will be familiar with the music that precedes it, called *Sailing By*. Played in full, it takes 2 minutes and 34 seconds. Usually there isn't enough time for this, so only 30 seconds or so are played. For many, the music and the Forecast go hand in hand, like the proverbial horse and carriage.

The original reason for having music before the Forecast was as a sort of alert to sailors to turn up the radio volume against, perhaps, the prevailing racket of adverse weather conditions outside, and make sure that pencil and paper were to hand.

Sailing By was composed by Ronald Binge, who was born in Derby in 1910. His father died in World War I and young Ronnie became the main breadwinner, supporting his mother and siblings by working in a gent's outfitters. But that was just a day job. He meanwhile served his musical apprenticeship in a rather dingy cinema, playing the piano and organ to accompany silent films.

He was also an accomplished accordionist, and played for a small orchestra at the cinema, which greatly improved his sight-reading skills as well as presenting many other musical challenges. By this time he was also interested in composition and soon mastered the complexities of orchestration.

Leaving Derby in 1932, he joined the John Russell Orchestra for a summer season in Great Yarmouth. Many of his colleagues recognised how talented he was and persuaded him to give London a try. It was very hard going at first, but slowly things started to look up, not least when he met a young Italian-born violinist who was looking for an accordionist for his orchestra. Ronnie got the job, not only as a player but also as the arranger. The violinist was none other than Mantovani, known the world over for his orchestral arrangements. Binge worked with him on the radio, in recording studios and on tours, and when time allowed he fitted in some writing, right up until the outbreak of World War II. He then joined the RAF, and during his active service he had his first major compositional hit with *Spitfire*, a tribute to the feisty fighter plane. He ran the RAF station choir along with a young Sidney Torch, who after the war went on to create the BBC show *Friday Night is Music Night* and conduct the BBC concert orchestra for many years. During the war, Binge also met his future wife Vera.

After the war, Binge gave up playing in favour of arranging and composing, again working with Mantovani. His 1952 arrangement of *Charmaine* created for the first time the novel 'sound' of cascading strings that quickly made the orchestra's popularity soar at home and abroad. The Mantovani Orchestra playing Ronald Binge's arrangements were the hot ticket of their day.

In spite of his successes, arranging piece after piece of other people's work eventually lost its charm for Binge, and he decided enough was enough. In 1952 he parted ways with Mantovani's orchestra to plough his own musical furrow.

It turned out to be a good decision, as two of his compositions during this period turned out to be overnight successes. The first was *Elizabethan Serenade*, which won him the Ivor Novello Award and had such international appeal that the added lyrics were translated into German, Norwegian, Swedish, Dutch, Danish and French. The second was *Sailing By*. In 1967 Jim Black, the Presentation Editor of Radio 4, chose it as the piece to precede the Shipping Forecast. It proved to be a remarkably enduring choice, even though it seems to be impossible to hum or whistle the melody – nobody knows why, but I know I can't.

The music caused a bit of a flurry in 1993 when the powers that be heard that the royalties paid for it were the equivalent of a staff member's salary. It was taken off the air until it was discovered that the information was wrong. This was some years after Ronald Binge's death in 1979; his music publisher and widow were suitably miffed at the BBC's cavalier treatment. However, everyone 'kissed and made up' when the misunderstanding was resolved and *Sailing By* has continued to sail by ever since.

EIGHT

—

SAILING BY THE SEAT
OF YOUR PANTS

Technology has changed the way we all work these days, but keeping a national radio network on the air with as few hiccups as humanly possible will always be a challenging occupation. Life is ruled by the clock – or perhaps that should be the clocks, liberally dotted around the studio, their relentless red second hands sweeping endless paths to the next minute or hour, always reminding you that you needed to be ready for whatever was next scheduled. All being well, this is the next 'junction', in other words the end of the current programme (be it live or recorded). This requires the announcer to tweak the script to sign off, and point to the next programme, before playing in a pre-recorded trail (or often a 'live' one) for a programme to be aired later. The idea is to keep everything running to time as smoothly as possible, and to make it all as interesting as you know how, while being warm, amiable and relaxed, and guiding the listener to hear a programme that they might not otherwise have thought of listening to.

In times gone by, on the other side of several sheets of glass – making your studio and the sound booth soundproof – you had the company of a Studio Manager or SM, whose job it was to balance the sound between items, and make sure that all the 'tapes' (as they were then) were in place and ready to be loaded onto hefty heavy-duty tape machines. These were 10-inch spools with about 2400 feet of tape on them, which would last about 38 minutes played at seven and a half inches per second. For an hour-long programme you needed two such reels, which involved the second reel being played in on a word cue, seamlessly, so that the 'change over' was undetected by the listener. If a tape had been heavily edited, it would literally have been cut and re-joined with special adhesive tape – so you had to cross your fingers that it would hold for the duration of the recording. On the rare occasions when a join came apart, the SM would become a blur of activity, feverishly trying (usually successfully) to save the day with a razor blade and new sticky tape. Meanwhile, the announcer opened the mic and calmly apologised for the technical fault that had suddenly and rudely interrupted whatever we had all been listening to. I say 'calmly'; well, you tried to sound calm, but your heart was thumping like a kettle drum, gallons of adrenaline were suddenly coursing through your veins, and you hoped upon hope that a resolution was soon at hand.

Once digital technology had been honed to near perfect reliability, all the main BBC radio networks, including Radio 4, began using it. This meant that we said goodbye to tapes and tape machines and, even more sadly, to the help and expertise of our SM colleagues. It was a case of *"Now you are on your own, chum."* New studios were built, each composed of several high-capacity computers. A new virtual play-out system was installed, the likes of 'moi' were given a few brief training sessions as to how it all worked, and then D-Day arrived. We had to select the recorded programmes from one of seven screens, balance our voice to the programmes, select the news summaries and all other live shows, make sure that the Pips appeared when they were wanted, which was largely at the top of each hour, and all manner of other technical things, as well as preparing our scripts and making the announcements. Someone once said that it was all rather like flying a helicopter, and although I haven't had that pleasure, I have been a passenger in one and can certainly see the parallels. It was also once likened to a swan cruising sedately down a river, while beneath the surface its legs were paddling like the clappers, giving the lie to the effortless appearance above water. By and large we all mastered the new technology, and my ex-colleagues continue to do so. There are aspects of the job that in all honesty I do not miss – not least the politics that are present in any organisation. However, when everything in the studio was going according to plan, your pre-calculated timings all came to fruition, your carefully timed script fitted the time available, and your hands landed on the right faders, it was all immensely rewarding.

Not everyone is happy working on their own, even with the knowledge that help is at hand a few seconds away in the main office should things go 'pear-shaped' without warning. I always found it a very peaceful environment, without the distractions of the hustle and bustle of an open-plan office a few yards away, many conversations taking place and phones ringing incessantly. The peace and quiet – apart from the two beefy high-quality studio loudspeakers – in the soundproof studio, made it the place to be, where you could concentrate on driving this national network. I altered the chair to the way I liked it, altered the lighting and heating ditto, and had everything laid out to my own way of working. Bliss.

That gives you an idea of some of the challenges faced both then and now by radio announcers in general, but reading the Shipping Forecast is like nothing else anyone has to read on the radio – real uncharted waters. Before you even get on air, there are one or two hurdles to get over: sometimes you have to wait with baited breath to get your hot little hands on the forecast. Even nowadays there can be an operational delay in sending the forecast through or a problem with the email's delivery, as it has to go through a number of servers at each end, any of which might choose that moment to throw a hissy fit and not work. Then when it arrives you have to check it's the right one, with no glaring errors in it or bits missing. These things can and do happen, despite the aid of computers, but not very often fortunately.

My early years of reading the Shipping Forecast were back in the 1970s, when technology was a bit more clunky than it is today – we're talking of the days of vinyl records, quarter-inch tape recorders, and something called 'cart machines', which were the bane of many people's lives. The one advantage of the cart machine was that they played quarter-inch cassettes on a loop with electronic tones (that are too high-pitched to be audible) on them to cue up and play in jingles etc. Fine if they worked, but a pain if they didn't. Cart machines were used a lot by DJs for their jingles. There was a time when *Sailing By* was recorded onto one of these quite large boxes, which you fed into the bowels of a 'cart player'. If the cart player worked, then all was wonderful, but if it didn't, then you had a problem. I seem to remember that we asked for a back-up copy for playing on a reel-to-reel machine – just in case. You laced up the leader tape and had the actual recording tape just short of the playback head. This was much more reliable than the cart machines and in the end it was what we usually used to play *Sailing By*. There was another problem waiting for the unwary. At least the cart machine used to cue up automatically (sometimes) whereas if you used the normal tape player you had to remember to cue it up yourself or you would be faced with an embarrassing silence. Avoiding this required accurate timing, or to be precise, back timing. As previously mentioned, *Sailing By* is two minutes 34 seconds long so you had to start it playing at exactly 0045 hours and 26 seconds, so that it would end in time for you to start reading the forecast at 0048 hours precisely. This meant you had to start it even though the preceding programme hadn't ended and then fade what is left when you had signed off that programme. I have to admit that I got caught out on occasion, either leaving me with unwanted time or having to fade the music out because I had started it late. Fun and games.

In those days the forecast came through on a very noisy and clapped-out teleprinter. The supposedly soundproof hat that was put on the machine to minimise the clackety noise it made when printing, had the effect of overheating it – which at worst would lead to failure of said machine to print, so you had to remember to remove the cover when expecting a forecast in order to prevent a malfunction! The other thing you had to remember was to keep an eye on the roll of paper inside the machine, which seemed to run out with ferocious frequency. On a bad day you would then discover that you had run out of spare rolls of paper too – panic stations! Quick scramble round to the studio next door to see if they could help out. Radio 3 would look at you a bit blankly and ask what a teleprinter was – "Oh no, we don't use those, Sorry." Too busy discussing Beethoven. Radio 2 were usually a better bet. Meanwhile, back in your studio, the message was still chuntering through but going nowhere, except round and round the cardboard roll upon which the paper had come. So, once you had found a new roll for the machine, you had to call the Met Office to ask them to send it again, which was sometimes met with derision. I am drawing a picture of the worst-case scenarios, but they did happen and it would set your heart pounding when time was against you. There were even some occasions when, for a mixture of reasons, you had to start reading the forecast before it was all delivered. On these occasions the Studio Manager (or Technical Operator, as they were way back then) would pop in as quietly as possible through

AND NOW THE SHIPPING FORECAST

the extremely heavy, lead-lined, soundproof doors to rip off the remainder of the electronic bog roll, again as quietly as possible, and pass it over to you at just the right moment. Now, when things were going smoothly you would have time to tear the very long sheet of paper into more manageable 'pages' to read from without too much paper shuffling noise. But with the late delivery scenario you could be handed a sheet of paper several feet long – which was something of a handful to say the least. Oh, the joys of live radio.

There were a few of my colleagues from years ago when the forecast was broadcast on Radio 2 (who shall remain nameless), who took the reading of the forecast a little less than seriously, shall we say. It was deeply worrying at the time but quite funny looking back now. One took it upon himself to try and set fire to the bottom of the forecast in the hands of some hapless newcomer. (Smoking was allowed of course in those days, and a very large number of us did, so matches and lighters were always to hand.) Such pranks never really jeopardised the forecast – there was always another copy to hand to replace the charred mess in the nick of time – just gave us some heart-stopping moments and certainly produced a rather strangulated delivery from the poor person being put through the mangle.

In the Radio 2 days there were not the time constraints that we faced after we switched to Radio 4. In fact there could be quite lengthy pauses between saying the sea areas etc., which two other Shipping Forecast readers cunningly managed to use to tell risqué stories to the engineer next door. They would alternately read a line of the forecast to the nation, then close down the microphone (or mic) and transfer to the talkback mic (the internal communication line with the engineer) to tell another line of the story. It required a cool mind and a degree of manual dexterity to accomplish this without mishap, but somehow – and I will never know how – they both got away with it for years. If I had tried it I'd have lost my place, lost the thread and most probably lost my job.

Sometimes on Radio 2 you had to read a News Summary directly after the Forecast. However, the Summary wouldn't be brought into the studio until you were at least halfway through the Forecast. A sub-editor from the newsroom, sometimes new to the job, would stumble in and place the News Summary pages within your reach. All being well it stayed put, but once it was disturbed by the draft from the heavy door as he left, and I noticed just too late to stop it fluttering gently and falling – out of reach – onto the floor. Three thoughts went through my mind at remarkable speed: would I be able to reach it in the nanoseconds I would have available, would the pages be numbered, and please, please could there NOT be any impossible names to pronounce that I hadn't had a chance to check.

For many years Jimmy Kingsbury was the boss of the Radio 2 announcers. You may well remember he presented *Friday Night Is Music Night* on Radio 2 for a long time before Robin Boyle took over. Jimmy was something of a perfectionist so was adamant that all those under his charge got everything right – not only the forecast, but news reading and indeed all else that the job required. He had a very good eye and ear when it came to selecting candidates for the job in the first place and then giving you the confidence you needed to do it well. He was an excellent teacher and would make you practice ad infinitum until you got the timing right. By the end of his training, you did get everything right, and it was all down to his patience and judgement. Many newsreaders have cause to be grateful to him. He built up a tight crew of bods who read the Forecast in the way he had taught them, so he was pretty mortified when Radio 4 took over long wave in the 1978 frequency changes, which meant the Forecast was moving to what he would have regarded as an alien network without the expertise to carry on the good work. He need not have worried, as several of those he had taught transferred to Radio 4 along with the Shipping Forecast. Amongst those were Iain Purdon, John Marsh, Peter Donaldson and myself – we did our best to keep the flag flying and pass on what we had learned to others over the following decades. I hope we all succeeded.

Although Radio 2 was a tightly run ship, there were still moments when things didn't go according to plan. Sometimes this was because of the frailty of individuals under pressure, sometimes because certain individuals would never ever buckle under what they saw as over-prescriptive management, but on other occasions it was purely down to the cock-up factor, which chooses a likely candidate for torture and then pounces.

There is a little worm that lies dormant in most broadcasters, and only comes to the fore on rare occasions, but when it does, the effect can be quite devastating. It manifests itself by the hard-to-resist urge to laugh (or 'corpse' to give it its stage name). It's all down to nerves really. You are under pressure, you are live on air, there are time limitations and you are human. Here is the story of an event that took place on Radio Scotland between a couple of pals of mine – Iain Purdon and Charles Nove, who later were to work on Radio 2 and Radio 4 respectively. Iain was reading the news; he had a slip of the tongue and although he spoonerised an item he thought he had retrieved the situation and not altered the newsroom's meaning too much. Then, as he embarked on the Fish Prices, made the mistake of letting his mind wander back to his error, and realised that it was really quite funny and he started to shake with suppressed laughter. Charles, sitting opposite him, knew exactly what was going on and decided to exit stage left, crawling out of the studio in an ape-like stance to collapse in hysterics as soon as he made it through the door. Unfortunately

Iain heard this and it finished him off – collapse of two stout parties and the listeners wondering what on earth had set them off. But this was not the end of the story. Iain had no means of closing his mic. The only person who could have done that had by now left the studio, and so Iain had to start reading the Inshore Waters Forecast in a state of near hysteria. He managed it but it took longer than planned as he had to keep stopping to try and compose himself. He recalls that one of the reports went something like: 'nine nine three…' (10-second pause while wiping tears from eyes) followed by… 'falling' in a quivering falsetto. The next day there was bit of an inquest and the News Editor made it known in no uncertain terms that he was less than pleased with what had happened. Luckily for all concerned, half a dozen newly qualified medics who were on the Isle of Skye celebrating their recent success heard the whole thing and wrote to the Head of Radio Scotland thanking him for the new comical approach to the Late News, Fish Report and Forecast. This was followed by another card the following day deploring the return of po-faced presentation. That intervention saved several rashers of bacon.

As you will have gathered, there are all manner of distractions that can swamp the most unshakeable and experienced of broadcasters with little or no warning. If you stop to think about the order of words that have come out of your mouth – particularly if they are wrong – it can have a hideous effect. I've made my share of slip-ups, one being referring to the Weather Forecast as the Feather Warcast – and yes, giggles did ensue.

On another personal note, a few years ago when my wife and I married, the Officiating Vicar wrote a brilliant piece. I will only quote a couple of lines as the rest was so pertinent to the day that it would mean little here. We were 60 and 57 respectively. It began: 'I won't ask Peter to play *Sailing By*, but I do have a Wedding

Forecast'. A little later he read, "Knuckles WIGHT, palms sweaty, hands joining to form new partnership, moderate, becoming good. FORTIES – you wish…" at which point the church erupted with laughter and applause for about half a minute before he could resume. You had to be there to get the full effect, but I'm sure you get the drift. It shows though how hard it is to escape from something that people associate you with.

NINE

—

A TALE OF SHIPPING
AREA TURBULENCE

PART ONE

I talked in Chapter Three about the reasons behind the names of the shipping areas, but have you ever thought about what else may have occurred in each area during this nation's maritime history? Some have fascinating tales to tell, so I'll spend this chapter and the next revealing more about what lies beneath the seemingly placid fabric that forms our island nation and its waters. We'll travel round in the normal Forecast order of course, from Viking down through the North Sea and English Channel, south to Trafalgar and then returning north around Ireland, until we eventually reach South East Iceland. By then, I hope your curiosity will have been satisfied by a plethora of lesser-known facts and figures about our shipping areas.

VIKING

—

The sea area to the west of Scandinavia bears testament to the seafaring prowess of the nearby inhabitants who criss-crossed these often hostile waters. The Vikings knew not only how to survive on long journeys with minimal food supplies on board (supplemented by fresh fish), but also understood the sea by observing how the birds above them were behaving, taking depth soundings and keeping an eye on what was floating by at any given time, all of which aided the small matter of navigation. They became more and more proficient, passing their skills down from father to son, and coupled with the excellent design of their craft, were leagues ahead of any other seafarers from those dark and distant times.

I had always assumed that the Vikings first landed in the British Isles on the coast of Scotland or north east England. In fact it appears that, when coming to see what the Saxons were made of, they made life even harder for themselves and travelled much further south, disembarking on the beach at Portland in Dorset in 789 AD, to the surprise and consternation of the locals. This first trip was a reconnaissance mission: farming was a thankless task in the Scandinavia of that time, so the Vikings were seeing if the British Isles were any more fertile. Portland gave them a taste of the comparative lushness to be found in the downlands of southern England. For many years there had been friendly trade, between the Vikings and their Scottish and British counterparts, but the Vikings became greedy, and thought, well why trade when if we attack and conquer, we can have it all for free. Having seen, if only briefly, that things looked much better this side of the North Sea, they began their assaults a few years later, particularly on the north of England, Scotland and also Ireland, and with increasing frequency and ferocity. Next came raids by hundreds of long ships sailing out of Denmark, and there was a big push in 851 A.D. when, with great daring, a huge contingent of Vikings swarmed up the Thames laying waste to both London and Canterbury in Kent in the process. Many battles ensued and the Vikings soon had control of a major part of the country between the Thames and Scotland. One area that managed to hold out was Wessex in south west

England, which was under the leadership of the young King Alfred. These torrid times changed the way our land was used and owned and affected our religious culture too. Norse languages have left a marked influence on our own, including giving us a lasting legacy in the form of place names the length and breadth of these islands.

The Vikings adventured not only to the British Isles but also to France and Spain, and across the Atlantic to Greenland and North America. It was an amazing feat that they managed to travel in their shallow draft boats, manned by up to 30 oarsmen (only later assisted by a single sail), across such huge distances. On the other hand, the shallow draft made river access relatively easy. Plenty of evidence has also been found that the Vikings followed the river networks deep inside Russia, founding settlements that have left remains to this day.

I live in Surrey close to the Thames and I once heard a local story that a Viking long ship lies buried near the river. It is said to have been found in 1937 by a workman digging the Desborough Cut, to make a shorter straighter journey, rather than following the meandering oxbow; this made it a shorter journey between Walton on Thames, Shepperton and Weybridge. The soil had somehow kept the ship in a remarkable condition so there was great excitement among archaeologists, who hoped to raise the vessel and put it on view somewhere for all to see in perpetuity. However, the storm clouds of war with Germany were about to break, and before the site could be surveyed, a stop was put to the work as money was now short. The part of the excavation that had laid bare the timbers of the long ship was covered over once more. It was hoped that after the war the dig would be resumed and the ship raised from its muddy resting place, but in the event this didn't happen. As far as I know the intriguing find is still there, unless the protective soil and mud over 70 years ago let enough oxygen in and around the timbers to rot them in the intervening years. I have to say that I haven't been able to verify this story – good though it is. However, a few years ago, what is thought to be a thousand-year-old Viking long ship was found under the foundations of a Merseyside pub car park. Once again, funding is required, as well as all the necessary permissions, to find out if it is the real McCoy.

THE UTSIRES

While there is nothing much to say about North Utsire, South Utsire is certainly worth a mention, as it seems to cover the area where the Battle of Jutland, the largest sea battle of World War I, took place. The British fleet had had some success in blockading the German fleet east of Denmark in the Skaggerak, preventing it from reaching the North Atlantic. A game of cat and mouse was played out on the afternoon of May 31st, 1916 as a total of 250 ships from both naval fleets tried to outwit each other. The battle raged until the sun set at about 2030. A total of 14 British ships and 11 German ones went down, with a considerable loss of life on both sides. Throughout the night the remaining British fleet tried to stop the German ships returning to the safety of port, with a view to continuing the battle the following morning at first light. This plan failed, however, with the German fleet making it back to port without any further engagement. Although both sides claimed victory, it was the British who had the heavier losses. Despite the battle, the Germans pressed on into the North Atlantic, where its threat to other shipping kept the Royal Navy busy. Germany was meanwhile pouring money and effort into submarine warfare, aiming to establish dominance under the waves. The speed of technological development meant that Germany could seek out and destroy merchant shipping in what later became known as the

First Battle of the Atlantic. The antagonism caused by these attacks on unarmed merchant ships was a key factor in persuading the USA to enter the war in 1917. By the outbreak of World War II, experience, tactics and hardware had all improved. In the Second Battle of the Atlantic the Germans inflicted an almighty toll on the merchant shipping bringing vital goods and foodstuffs to the beleaguered UK and also to her Soviet ally. The clock was ticking though, and the Western Allies secured the shipping lanes against surface attack in 1941 and against the U-boats two years later – but that's another story.

FORTIES

The Germans were also active around our next sea area, Forties. At the end of World War I in 1918 the most powerful ships of the German High Sea Fleet surrendered to the Royal Navy's Admiral Beatty off the Firth of Forth. This came after the Allied victory on land, and wouldn't have been possible were it not for the Allied command of the waves.

So we move on properly to Forties. This sea area contains many of the North Sea's oil and gas fields, and the weather forecasts for this area are of utmost importance to those aboard the various fixed oil-drilling platforms. The Forties Oil Field, just over 100 miles east of Aberdeen, is named after the sea area. The first rigs were similar in terms of construction to the World War II Maunsell Sea Forts that had been erected to act as anti-aircraft batteries in the Thames and Mersey estuaries (see THAMES later in this chapter). Once the rigs had been built onshore, they were towed out to sea, tipped onto their 'feet' and secured to the seabed. The field produced oil from 1975 until 2003, when its output declined and BP sold it to the American Apache Corporation. Then of course there is also the

Piper Oil Field. Its Piper Alpha platform began oil production in 1976, later converting to gas production, and accounted for 10% of North Sea production at its peak. However, on July 6th, 1988 an explosion sparked a fire that destroyed BP's rig, killing 167 men with only 59 survivors. The financial loss was put at about £1.7 billion. It was one of the worst ever offshore oil disasters in terms of lives lost and impact on the oil and gas industry – a gloomy point in the quest for riches in the North Sea, underlining the enormous risks that workers take on these isolated rigs.

CROMARTY

Sea area Cromarty is named after the town of the same name, which goes way back to the thirteenth century, when it was a Royal Burgh giving it permission to trade. It had its own castle and was very prosperous for a while until – along with most of the north of Scotland – it suffered hard times for the following hundred years. Trade improved in the early 1600s and more or less continued to do so right through to the nineteenth century with income from fishing and then in the last century with the naval base created at Cromarty Firth which was soon recognised as one of the best natural harbours in Europe.

The Sutors of Cromarty, on the southern headland, are the east and west headlands at the entrance of Cromarty Firth. The entrance was guarded by substantial gun emplacements atop the North and South Sutors. Sutor which is the Scots word for 'shoemaker' was to spawn all manner of legends one of which included the two 'Sutors' as giant shoemakers who threw their tools back and forth across the Firth. All quite amicable apparently.

Cromarty Firth became a heavily used Royal Navy anchorage

during World War I. To protect the fleet very extensive defences were put in place including booms and a minefield to ward off enemy U-Boats. These protective devices were also put to use, although to a lesser extent during World War II. This was because the base was uncomfortably near commonly used German Luftwaffe routes and was thought to have been a potentially tempting target if they had been so minded. The base was finally abandoned in the 1950s and remained unused for the following twenty years or so. In the 1970s, this deep water port was brought back to life with the advent of the offshore oil and gas industries and has remained in use by them ever since. Also of importance here is the Cromarty Firth Port Authority, which offers deep-water berths and tailor made cargo-handling facilities – and it is also the primary port for the inspection, maintenance and repair of the North Sea Oil Rigs.

FORTH

The Firth of Forth has the dubious distinction, if that is the word, of being the first place in the UK to see enemy action in October 1939 soon after the outbreak of World War II. Royal Naval ships anchored not far from the Forth Railway Bridge were bombed by a squadron of Junkers Ju 88s. However what had attracted the Lufwaffe was HMS *Hood* – the pride of the Royal Navy's battleships seen steaming towards the Firth of Forth, heading for the Rosyth naval base. HMS *Hood* made it into the dockyard before the Junkers arrived. However, at this very early stage in the war Hitler had ordered that there should be no civilian casualties so HMS *Hood* on this occasion was spared and the German bombers turned their attack instead on the ships near the railway bridge. Two ships were hit, firstly HMS *Southampton* which got away with comparatively light damage even though a bomb passed through her superstructure and two decks before exploding in the sea. HMS *Mohawk* fared less well. A five hundred pound bomb exploded in the sea right by her side and the force of the explosion lifted her stern right out of the water and caused a shower of shrapnel propelled with such force, that it penetrated the quarter inch armour plating along the whole of one side of the ship. On the bridge the Commander Richard Jolly, although mortally wounded, refused medical help, and kept control of his vessel and saw it back to port before dying from his injuries. Another reputed first that day was the shooting down of one of the Junkers Bombers by a Spitfire – the first Spitfire *kill* of the war.

In 2008 a World War II bomb was detected on the sea bed of the Firth of Forth and was the cause of some concern. In came the Royal Navy's Northern Diving Group to deal with it. Many decades of corrosion made it a tricky proposition to handle, but after a while it was made safe before being destroyed where it lay. It is quite often deep sea fishermen who discover these dangerous relics from all those years ago and what seems to be a fine heavy catch of fish soon turns out to be something far less appealing and often highly dangerous.

TYNE

Following the coast southward we reach Tyne. The area of north east England around the River Tyne, has a great history of shipbuilding. In the early 20th century there was an almost insatiable demand for the production of warships and repair facilities. Swan Hunter was one of the famous yards, producing ships such as the *Mauretania* (1906) and then the *Carpathia* (1912), which braved the icebergs to rescue survivors of the *Titanic*. The area prospered until the Great Depression of the early 1930s caused huge cuts in orders, resulting in massive job losses in the yards, with Jarrow being the worst affected.

The onset of another war revived the fortunes of the shipyards, with many rush orders for military shipping, but by the 1960s the English yards were struggling to compete for new orders with the cheaper costs of overseas shipbuilders, especially those in Japan and the Far East. In all they built some 1600 vessels including cargo liners, ferries, destroyers, frigates and submarines.

DOGGER

As I mentioned earlier, Dogger is named after Dogger Bank – no, not a canine financial institution, but a huge sandbank that lies under a large shallow area in the North Sea. It is thought that in the Ice Age this formed a land bridge between Britain and the continent. When the ice melted, the bridge was submerged.

One other thing to say before moving on to some of the naval events that took place here, is that under this sandbank in 1931 there was the largest earthquake ever recorded in the British Isles, measuring 6.1 on the Richter Scale. The shockwaves were felt in the UK, Belgium and France, with some damage caused to buildings down the east side of England, although no deaths or injuries were reported. Talking of earthquakes, I have only experienced two. The first one was merely a very mild tremor: it was a few years ago, in 2002, and I was reading my book in bed one night when there was a thump, sounding rather like a door slamming in the neighbour's house, and the lampshade trembled. Funny, I thought. The next day there was a news item about a tremor in the Midlands, almost 150 miles away. The time matched exactly what I had heard and seen about 12 hours earlier. My second experience was rather more dramatic and took place on the island of Rhodes in 2008. My wife and I had a rather rude awakening at about 0630 one morning by the weirdest noise. Our room (which was 11 floors up) was starting to sway – my wife's first thoughts were that I was having fit or something, though I'm not sure why. She tried getting out of bed, but was thrown back onto it, at which point she suddenly realised that she too was being shaken around. The wardrobe moved away from the wall, the drawers began to come out of the chest. My wife asked what we should do. I said we should stay put as it would soon be over. I had my fingers crossed under the bedclothes – as that is where I had remained. (Was it true British stiff upper lip or was I paralysed by fear? I leave you to judge.) Then the air conditioning went off, as the power had been cut. The grinding, roaring noise grew still louder, the lurching of the building was nothing short of terrifying, and I was having visions of us going down to breakfast the quick way atop a mound of rubble. But just as quickly as it had started, the noise and movement subsided and we stared at each other. 'Bloody Hell!' I exclaimed, 'I always wondered what an earthquake would feel like. Now I know, and one's enough thank you.' A few minutes later the power came back on and we switched on the TV to see what Sky News had to say. Right away up came the caption at the bottom of the screen saying that an earthquake with a magnitude of 6.3 had just been reported under the sea just off Rhodes, with no immediate reports of damage or casualties. We later learned that a local woman, fearing for her life, had run out of her house, slipped and fallen down some steps, breaking her neck. So sad, as if she had stayed put she would have been unharmed. Half an hour after the quake, once we had regained our composure or whatever it is you do after such an extraordinary experience, we went down to a very early breakfast. We were not the only ones to venture out in search of reassurance, and you can imagine what the sole topic of conversation was, with all of us talking like old friends although in fact we were complete strangers. Sorry for the digression, now where was I…

Dogger Bank has witnessed a number of naval battles over the centuries. In 1781, during the American War of Independence (cup of tea anyone), the Dutch Republic, who along with France had been supporting the Americans for a long time, took exception to the British blockading the Dutch coast in order to stop supply ships heading for America. The Dutch attempted to get a merchant fleet through the British blockade, and on August 5th, 1781 there took place over the course of about three hours a rather inconclusive sea battle with quite heavy loss of life. While the Dutch claimed victory, they didn't try to leave port again except for one convoy that they managed to smuggle out under Swedish flags. Thus ended the brief (first) Battle of Dogger Bank.

This though didn't end the string of incidents in this sea area. If what I am about to tell you had not been so serious, it would be funny. We are now in the early 20th century at the time of the Russo-Japanese War. On October 21st, 1904 a group of Russian warships – their Baltic Fleet – were heading for the Far East to take part in the conflict there. The Russians heard reports of Japanese torpedo boats in the Dogger Bank area, as well as submarines and even minefields in the North Sea, but these in fact turned out to be spurious. However, these reports made the Russians very nervous, and an order was issued to the effect that it was imperative that no vessel of any kind whatever was to be permitted to get amongst the fleet. The incident that ensued began because the drunken captain of a fleet support ship thought that a passing Swedish ship was in fact a Japanese torpedo boat, and furthermore imagined through his drunken stupor that his vessel was being attacked by this supposed torpedo boat. What followed was close to farce. The Russians mistakenly identified a harmless collection of 30 British trawlers as more Japanese torpedo boats and opened fire on them, killing a handful of trawler men. Then some of the Russian ships began firing on each other. The only thing that saved the whole incident from becoming an even worse tragedy, with a far higher number of casualties, was the very poor quality of the artillery crews aboard the Russian ships – it was reported that one ship let loose 500 rounds without hitting a thing. Not surprisingly the Dogger Bank Incident created something of a diplomatic flurry between Russia and the UK – which was eventually resolved, although not without some difficulty – not least because there was an Anglo-Japanese alliance in force at the time.

We now move forward to World War I and January 24th, 1915 for another Battle of Dogger Bank. But first of all I need to give you the background to the event. In the Battle of Heligoland Bight the previous August, four German ships had been sunk without loss to the British (though two of our ships were very badly damaged and had to be towed back to port for extensive repairs). This success had been achieved despite there having been once again rather too much communication confusion and a general lack of planning. Nonetheless, the end result was that British ships remained in the area, preventing further sorties by the German fleet. Well, that was the idea anyway. However, the Germans clearly hadn't seen the script: having been unable to take any action for some time, frustration got the better of them and they broke free. On reaching the north east coast of England, they began to shell the towns of Scarborough, Whitby and Hartlepool, killing and wounding some 630 civilians. The raiding party left and were chased by British ships but the combination of adverse weather conditions and once again severe communications problems between our ships allowed the Germans to escape.

This brings us to the Battle of Dogger Bank. After their perceived success, the next target for the German fleet was the British fishing fleet on Dogger Bank. The British seem to have got their act together for this one, as some German radio signals were intercepted and decoded by British Naval Intelligence thus compromising the

Germans without their knowledge. So, at the allotted hour when the German fleet thought they were going to have things all their own way again – this time decimating the unarmed British Fishing Fleet going about their lawful business – they were taken a bit off guard when the Royal Navy turned up in strength. A high-speed chase ensued with both sides firing their guns at the very limit of their ranges. Each side took casualties, both in terms of ships damaged and lives lost. We lost 11 men and had two ships towed home. However the Germans lost 951 men, most of these casualties occurring when one of their ships was sunk. Unbelievably there were once again some signalling errors between our ships, which later resulted in certain senior officers being relieved of their duties. Although this battle was not hugely important in itself, it did give a much needed boost to British morale.

More recently, in September 1966, a World War II German U-boat, which had been scuttled in 1945 and then was raised, re-furbished and re-commissioned, came to grief on the Dogger Bank in a gale, with the loss of all but one of her 20-man crew. This was one of the highest losses of life suffered in peacetime by the German Navy.

Even more recently, a license was granted in early 2010 for a wind farm to be developed in the Dogger Bank, although construction work is not expected to start until at least 2014. The subjects of climate change and global warming are something of a hot potato at the moment and will probably remain so for quite a while. What one can say with some certainty is that there have always been periods of climatic change since this planet came into being, and there always will be until our sun dies and we go with it. There seems to be no international cohesion in tackling the disciplines involved spanning oceanography, meteorology and ecology, and until there is, everyone will continue to pull in different directions. I am something of a sceptic as to how much we puny human beings may or may not be influencing the world's weather patterns and temperatures. The might of nature is so much greater than anything we can do and I think that even en masse, and clever though man can be, there is something very arrogant in the make-up of homo sapiens that makes him think he can make a jot of difference in the long run. Do not think that I am advocating that we do nothing, but we should not kid ourselves that in the end we will make very much, if any, difference. The mention above of the wind farm sparked off my little rant, and it is true that we should certainly let nature help us when we can engineer it, although the worth of acres upon acres of massive great propellers – be they out at sea, with the hazards that may cause, or on dry land, where they take up huge tracts of land and are to my mind something of an eyesore – is a moot point. Only time will tell I suppose.

GERMAN BIGHT

The German Bight nestles in the curve of the north coast of mainland Europe between Denmark, Germany and the Netherlands. We called this sea area Heligoland until 1955, but then it was renamed to match the name used by the countries that border it, namely German Bight. The inhabitants of this coastline have struggled for centuries with the encroaching tides, as indeed have those along parts of the east coast of the British Isles. Amazing land reclamation has taken place, in the Netherlands in particular – certainly a tribute to the ingenuity of man, although I can't help feeling that the difference it has made, real though it is, is very fragile. The Germans and Danes too have dug dykes but have a little more natural protection from some fairly substantial sand dunes that are, for the most part, above the normal high tide level. There have been some pretty large storm surges over the past 40 years, which have given rise to fears of tidal inundation and a threat not only to life and limb but to large agricultural areas, vital for food production and economic activity.

HUMBER
—

Moving on, we now arrive at the Humber sea area, named after the large estuary formed by the Trent and Ouse rivers on the east coast between Lincolnshire and Yorkshire. The estuary's best-known feature is the single-span suspension bridge, which had a somewhat long gestation period before it was eventually 'born' in 1981. A bridge was badly needed and had been talked about for nearly a hundred years, to aid trade and cut travel times between Hull and Grimsby by almost 50 miles. Even when agreement was reached on building it in the 1950s, there followed a long wrangle as to who was going to finance it, so construction did not begin until 1972. Since opening, the bridge has made a huge impact on the area, with economic development on both sides proceeding in a far more unified fashion. There are now chemical works, power stations and oil refineries, and the two ports handle something like 14% of the UK's international trade. For the first 16 years of its life it had the added cachet of being the world's longest single-span suspension bridge, spanning 1410 metres, and although subsequently surpassed, it still ranks fifth in the world.

The Humber Lifeboat Station at Spurn Point is now the only one in the country with a full-time crew. It celebrated its 200th anniversary in 2010 and has recorded some incredible rescues during these two centuries. In particular, the station's legendary coxswain Robert Cross earned an impressive collection of RNLI medals – two gold, three silver, two bronze and the George Medal – for his feats of bravery between 1912 and 1943.

THAMES

Our next port of call is the Thames sea area, spanning the estuary of what is probably the UK's best-known river – although I'm sure there are those who will contest this. For centuries, the mudflats on the northern side of the estuary were a popular place for smugglers to land contraband. Rich pickings and cut-price bargains were up for grabs, without HM Customs taking their slice first. Canvey Island was a prime spot: not a very healthy place, but largely unpopulated – except by sheep and they weren't going to snitch on anyone, as to do so would have been strictly non-Ewe.

During World War II, London was protected to some extent – though of course not fully – from the marauding German bombers by a series of fortified towers called the Thames Estuary Forts or Maunsell Sea Forts. These were hastily erected, with some difficulty, in the estuary and armed with anti-aircraft batteries to catch the German bombers as they flew in low to avoid radar detection. The forts had some moderate success but not as much as had been hoped. The Government decommissioned them in the late 1950s, and they hit the headlines again in the mid-1960s when pirate radio stations inhabited them. That only lasted until the 1967 Marine and Broadcasting Offences Act forced them to close down.

I was briefly at Cliftonville boarding school, near Margate, in the early 1950s. One night on the cusp of January and February 1953 there was the mother and father of a storm, which blew down the whole of the east coast of England, causing huge amounts of flooding as the sea, whipped up by the wind, inundated many coastal areas and treated the coastal defences as though they didn't exist. Over 300 people in England died that night, around 24,000 homes were flooded and 30,000 people were left homeless. One of the casualties of this storm was the 140-year-old Margate lighthouse:

its foundations were sucked out from under it by the fierce tides kicked up by the storm, coupled with the ferocious wind. I remember the next day I was there amongst a crocodile of young boys being taken down to see...well nothing really. It was pointed out to us that this was where, until the previous night, a lighthouse had stood. As I think none of us had ever seen or noticed it, it didn't exactly inspire us in the same way that it did the local adults of the area, who were probably and rightly shocked and amazed. The storm not only hit England, but had also torn down the Dutch coast, causing much more serious damage there with over 1800 deaths that night. Parts of France, Belgium and Denmark were also affected. The storm also magnified the high spring tides, which rose something like three metres above the normal high-tide level.

DOVER

—

Next we move down to the Dover sea area, or Pas-de-Calais as it is known in the French bulletins. By its very closeness to the French coast, this strip of water has always been of prime strategic importance. In more recent times we think of course of the two world wars, but long before that both the town and Strait of Dover were very important for our national defence. Cap Gris Nez, near Calais, is a mere 21 miles away from the English shore, and on a fine day you can see the glass glinting in the church in Calais's main square from anywhere along this stretch of the English coast. The Strait of Dover is the busiest international seaway in the world – quite a claim these days, but it's true. A very large percentage of the maritime traffic sailing from the Atlantic to either the North or Baltic Seas uses this narrow route in preference to the far more dangerous passage round the north of Scotland. The mix of vessels, from single small boats to ocean-going liners, freighters and tankers, make for a hazardous collection of hardware tick-tacking through the Strait 24 hours a day, 365 days a year. Safety is paramount, and to this end HM Coastguard maintains a constant watch on all shipping movements, be they large or small. The added problem is that on top of the high volume of east-west traffic, there is also much north-south traffic, as cross-channel ferries and private sailing craft ply back and forth, making the potential risk of collision that much higher. Anyway, let's go back, if not to the beginning, then certainly a few millennia.

About 6000 years ago Stone Age farmers crossed by boat from France and set up home, raising crops and children, in and around what is now Dover. There then seems a bit of a knowledge gap as next to be knocking on Dover's door was Julius Caesar, who also used the shortest possible crossing from what was then the edge of the Roman Empire in Gaul (France) to see what was on offer in these isles. Dover, or as it was then known Dubris, had an attractive harbour (by which I mean that it was a safe haven from the weather – nobody could ever claim that Dover Harbour was in any way attractive in the sense of being good to look at). As his ships approached, he spied the rather hostile white cliffs and some even more hostile heavily armed men standing atop of them. Hmm, change of plan then. So he popped further along the coast to see if things were any easier there. And so it came to pass that on August 26th, 55 BC the Romans first landed in the British Isles, running their ships onto the shingle beaches at Walmer (which also happens to be the town where I lived as a small boy). It's not clear whether this was an attempt at an invasion or merely a reconnaissance mission. There was no doubt the following year though, when about 800 ships landed at the same spot on the Kent coast and established a foothold – this must have been a very intimidating sight for the Britons. The landing was not without incident though, as the Roman sailors were not used to the storms that could crash through the Strait of Dover – being more used to the calmer

Mediterranean waters – and a few dozen boats were badly damaged at anchor. This, and the previous year's landing, turned out to be intelligence-gathering enterprises – the main aim of the Romans was always to gather booty, such as gold, silver and jewels, but they soon realised that such riches were not to be found in these lands. So for the next century the greedy Roman Empire focused its resources on raping and pillaging other parts of Europe and north Africa, and it wasn't until 43 AD that Emperor Claudius began the permanent conquest of Britain.

Dover Castle, on its perch overlooking the Channel, is a mighty structure. Fortification on this site almost pre-dates history itself, and it has been developed extensively for strategic and defensive purposes over the centuries. There is evidence of ramparts dating back to the Iron Age and then the Romans constructed a lighthouse or *pharos* in 1 AD. The Saxons built a fortified town or *burgh*, although all that remains is a 10th-century church. The majority of the masonry that we see today dates back no further than about the 12th century, but this is no mean achievement nonetheless – they don't build them like that anymore. So good was the castle's construction that no further additions of any note were made until the 1740s. Both the Georgians and Victorians then decided that the place needed a bit of sprucing up inside and out: some walls were lowered to make artillery positions facing out to sea and the outer walls were strengthened.

In 1909 Louis Blériot made the first flight across the Channel, from Calais to Dover – a clear signal that the Channel could no longer be regarded as a nice, safe, protective moat, shielding us from invasion from Europe. The castle would, nevertheless, play an important role in both world wars. During World War I the Royal Navy was in charge of all shipping movements in and out of the harbour below the castle. This had become even more important given the greatly increased use of submarines instead of surface vessels by the Germans – what needed to be done urgently was to discover the location of the U-boat bases so that they could be rooted out and the craft destroyed. In 1918, the Dover Patrol conducted the Zeebrugge Raid against the U-boat base discovered in the harbour there. It was well planned, but ended up blocking the U-boats in port for only a few days. Before the end of that war, German bombers were flying across the Channel; they were met with very powerful searchlights and anti-aircraft fire from the castle battlements.

During World War II, use was made of the tunnels that had been dug into the cliffs in Napoleonic times, to create a bombproof HQ for the British High Command of the area. Important though that was, many say that the castle's finest hour in recent times came in May 1940 when Hitler's armies were marching westwards across Europe and within three weeks had forced their way between the British and French armies, leaving about 400,000 troops trapped on the Dunkirk beaches. More on this a bit later, but suffice to say that within Dover Castle a unit was rapidly formed to organise an evacuation of unprecedented size and complexity. It was a huge task, and the Castle can lay claim to being at the forefront of that effort. In February 1942, three German battle cruisers, the *Scharnhorst, Gneisenau* and *Prinz Eugen,* which had been holed up in the French port of Brest for safety after the sinking of the *Bismarck* the year before, were instructed by the German High Command to head urgently for Norway, where an invasion was feared. Their shortest route was of course along the English Channel. This was to be a daring if not audacious dash – but it turned out that luck and human error were on their side. The discovery that the ships had left Brest was not made until the following morning. Among the British vessels scrambled to give chase up the Channel, heading for the North Sea, were five motor torpedo boats from Dover, which duly attacked but failed in their mission of interception, as did other Royal Navy vessels and the RAF. This was not our finest hour: it was the first time that a hostile fleet had sailed through the English Channel since the Spanish Armada. The difference this time was that the German fleet made good their escape.

By the end of the Cold War – during which, if there had been a nuclear war, this complex would have become a regional centre of government – the Castle was finally decommissioned. Today it plays host to tourists as a 'must see' attraction.

Dover is one of the Cinque Ports, a confederation set up during the reign of Edward the Confessor in or around 1050 under which Hastings, Romney, Hythe, Dover and Sandwich took on what was called 'Ship Service'. This was an arrangement between these five towns and the monarch whereby they received special royal privileges in return for providing ships and men to him for free for 15 days a year. This was quite a big ask, and by the 12th century the original ports found themselves unable to support the Crown in this way without extra help. Arrangements were made to include Winchelsea and Rye, which became head ports, and other towns joined later as 'limbs' or 'members' serving under a head port.

The Portsmen, as they were known, had the most extraordinarily powerful rights under this arrangement. They had free reign over tax and legal matters, which including their own courts, judges, tolls and free salvage rights from all shipwrecks found at sea or onshore. This made them both rich and also very hard to control. It was a huge amount of self-regulated power to have been given in those days. Eventually something had to be done to curb the accrued power of the Portsmen: enter the Lord Warden of the Cinque Ports. From the early 13th century whoever held this post (an appointment for life made by the monarch in recognition of faithful service to the Crown) also held the post of Constable of Dover Castle. It was not an easy job in the early days as the Lord Warden somehow had to represent the best interests of both the monarch and the Portsmen – which were sometimes at odds with one another to put it mildly. In recent history holders of this post have included Sir Winston Churchill, Sir Robert Menzies and HM Queen Elizabeth, the Queen Mother. The installation ceremony of a new Lord Warden used to take place in the remains of the Roman lighthouse, but more recently they have been held at the ancient Priory of St Martin within the grounds of Dover College. Since 1708 the official residence of the Lord Warden has been Walmer Castle, very near where my family used to live. The Castle was transformed into a comfortable country house estate by successive Wardens, and I have to say the gardens are spectacular. My grandmother's ashes were quietly spread there some years ago, according to her wishes, and I can understand her reasons for requesting this. Amongst former wardens was the Duke of Wellington, who died there. My grandmother once had a quiet word with the man who was in charge of Wellington's room, the red rope was raised and I was allowed to go and sit on his favourite chair, which made this little boy's day, I can tell you – a case of *Wow!*

The Cinque Ports were undoubtedly at their peak in the 13th century, but the temptations put in the way of the Portsmen by the huge powers they had been granted led to, shall we say, some very dubious and dishonest activities. In the next century nature stamped its own mark on the arrangement, as some of the ports ceased to be navigable or even became completely landlocked. In 1588 the curtain came down after the final act carried out by the Cinque Ports Fleet against the Spanish Armada – not a bad way to go out.

The pretty and ancient town of Sandwich, another of the Cinque

Ports, used to be on the coast but is now some two miles inland due to centuries of silting in and around the mouth of the River Stour. It is hard to imagine that it had a harbour large enough to hold both trading and warships in times gone by – but unfortunately it was also large enough to attract invading warships from France. On one occasion in 1457 the town was attacked by about 4000 Frenchmen who had sailed over from Honfleur. Many citizens were killed including the town's Mayor. To commemorate this event the Mayor of Sandwich still wears a black robe to this day, but I'm pleased to report that relations between Sandwich and Honfleur have been repaired. It is hard when mentioning Sandwich not to think of the convenient food that so many of us ply ourselves with on a fairly regular basis. The most likely reason for the sandwich being so-called goes back to a certain John Montagu, fourth Earl of Sandwich. In about 1762 he was in the middle of a gambling game (unspecified) and requested that some meat be placed between two slices of bread to help sustain him during his endeavours. The story is probably apocryphal, but it's a nice one. The Earls of Sandwich had no connection with the town, apart from the title. In fact in 1660 the first Earl, Edward Montagu, was going to take the title of the Earl of Portsmouth, but instead (perhaps because the fleet he was commanding at the time was lying off Sandwich) he decided to take the title of Sandwich. This fleet was waiting for the *green light* to go and collect Charles II from his enforced exile in France. All a bit strange: if the Earl had gone for the Portsmouth title we would now be ordering BLT Portsmouths, which doesn't have quite the same ring to it.

The Strait of Dover deserves one final mention, and this is in connection with the infamous Channel Tunnel. I say infamous only because of the time it took to get the thing dug and ready for use. While I daresay whole books have been written on the subject, I'm just going to add a few lines. The idea of a tunnel was first mooted, staggeringly, as far back as 1802, although fears that such a project would be a threat to national security scuppered the idea. At that time, the Channel was still seen as a secure defence against European attack, so building a tunnel could provide free access on a plate. It wasn't until 182 years later that the Eurotunnel company began construction and the Chunnel was opened in 1994. The initial downside of the project was the huge overspend – it ended up costing around 80% more than the original estimate. Other problems were to follow, including fires, illegal immigrants and asylum seekers. At the moment it still holds the record for having the longest undersea section of any tunnel in the world. I myself have yet to use it, but in spite of its many problems, I look forward to climbing aboard one day in London and emerging at the Gare du Nord in Paris for a wander around one of my favourite cities.

Times change, and something that probably made thousands of people choke on their cornflakes in early 2010 was the *Daily Mail* headline proclaiming *"White Cliffs of Dover to be sold to the French to help reduce Government's debt."* On reading the article, the actual story was seen to be slightly less contentious, but only slightly. What was actually being proposed was the sale of the Port of Dover to the French authorities, as privatisation would provide the funding to expand the port and build the second terminal necessary to improve its profitability. (The Port of Dover is the largest British port still in public ownership.) All this was prior to the 2010 general election, and therefore before the Tory/Lib-Dem alliance took over the reins in Downing Street. Possibly they will have other ideas, although there is still a hefty national debt to pay off, so who knows.

We have many other sea areas to go, but we will stay in this one a bit longer as we head a little further back up the coast to previously mentioned Walmer. As a four-year old boy, I remember being very worried about a mine that was mounted on the foreshore at

Walmer. This was only about four years after the end of World War II. I had been told what mines were for and that when one went off at sea when hit by a ship, it made a very loud bang and did a lot of damage. I didn't altogether believe that this one had been emptied of its high explosives and made completely harmless, so I always gave it a wide berth when being walked along the seafront by my mother, who was constantly amused at my obvious nervousness caused by this alien object.

The RNLI lifeboats at Walmer and nearby Deal have been kept very busy over the years. I remember seeing both of them being launched on several occasions to go to the aid of those in trouble on the often very rough seas here in the Dover Strait. Such was the impact on my young mind of the bravery of these men, who were usually working voluntarily in the most frightful and dangerous weather conditions, that to this day the RNLI is one of the few charities to which I subscribe.

Apart from the storms that can blow up here, there is the added and very real hazard of the lethal and ever-shifting Goodwin Sands – or the 'Ship Swallower' as it is known locally. The sandbank is about four miles offshore and stretches for about nine miles from Kingsdown to Pegwell Bay, just south of Ramsgate. When the tide goes out, a large part of the Sands are exposed to the air, drying quite quickly and becoming quite hard. There have even been games of cricket held on them, although they must have been quite short ones, as once the tide returns, hasty evacuation is not only advised but mandatory before the firm sand once more turns to quicksand and sucks you into oblivion. *HOWZAT!*

Well over 2000 ships have been wrecked here, resulting in the loss of goodness knows how many lives, and it is for this reason that there are two lifeboat stations in very close proximity to the

Goodwins. An area of deep water off Pegwell Bay provides a relatively safe anchorage from the strong easterly or westerly winds that can occur here, but as many a sailor has discovered to his cost, if the storm is violent enough to break a ship's moorings, the vessel could get swept onto the sands, which even at high tide will catch out all but the shallowest of them. Once a craft has hit the sandbank there is usually only one outcome, and that is the total loss of it and any cargo on board. Most ships are claimed by the quicksand within a few hours – only the rapid evacuation of the crew onto its own lifeboats plus help from the RNLI prevents loss of life too.

The Sands do have a very grisly record. The first accounted loss was a merchant ship en route from Flanders in 1298. (Many must have perished before this date, but the records, if kept, haven't survived.) In 1689 the 50-gun HM *Frigate Sedgemore*, supposedly carrying the vast wealth (in those days) of £200,000, got stuck on the sands. No treasure from her was ever found but there is a good chance that deep in the sands many other precious cargoes are lurking, probably never to be recovered. The most calamitous single loss of life occurred during the Great Storm of 1703 when the Sands claimed 13 men-o'-war amongst many other vessels, causing the huge deaths of over 2000 sailors. The first steamship to be caught out was the SS Violet in 1857. A World War I casualty was the German U-boat U48, which was first shelled and then chased onto the banks. The crew were forced to surrender and once the tide came back in it vanished. Strangely is has reappeared from time to time, the most recent occasion being in 1973. When I was young I remember seeing a wreck on the Sands, which was probably either the *Luray Victory*, which ran aground in 1946, or its sister ship, the *North Eastern Victory*, which foundered a year later. Both broke their backs but were not swallowed by the sand – their masts were still visible towards the end of the 20th century. The

MV *Ross Revenge*, which hosted the pirate radio station *Radio Caroline*, drifted onto the sand in 1991, thereby ending the offshore era of pirate radio in the UK.

The first lightship dropped anchor in 1795, to warn passing vessels away from the extreme danger of the Sands. Another was positioned in 1809 with a further two added in 1832 and 1874. However, even these lightships did not escape the ravages of the Goodwins: in 1954 the South Goodwin lightship was wrecked with the loss of all seven crew. There remains just one lightship now, the East Goodwin, as the other lightships have been replaced with unmanned automatic beacons. The advent of GPS navigation systems has greatly improved vessels chances of getting safely round the Goodwins, and it is felt that with this modern technology the Sands may at last cease to be the danger they once were. If you do find yourself at sea in this area though, just spare a thought for those who perished – and make sure you are able to steer a safe course yourself.

The notoriety of the Sands has inspired a few literary mentions across the centuries. In Shakespeare's *The Merchant of Venice* we come across the following:

> *Why, yet it lives there uncheck'd that Antonio hath a ship of rich lading wrecked on the narrow seas; the Goodwins, I think they call the place; a very dangerous flat and fatal, where the carcasses of many a tall ship lie buried, as they say, if my gossip Report be an honest woman of her word.*

Then we find written in Herman Melville's *Moby Dick*:

> *In what census of living creatures, the dead of mankind are included; why it is that a universal proverb says of them, that they tell no tales, though containing more secrets that the Goodwin Sands.*

There is also a reference to the Sands in Ian Fleming's James Bond novel *Moonraker*, and he also made them an important part of the plot in his children's story *Chitty Chitty Bang Bang*. I suspect that Fleming got many of the ideas for his Bond stories from his World War II experiences in Naval Intelligence. It's also interesting to note that Ian Fleming had a house a short distance away from the Sands at St. Margaret's Bay.

Just before we move round the coast into the English Channel in the next chapter, I'll mention an interesting geological discovery relating to this whole area. Some 450,000 years ago, a prehistoric river flowed through the Strait of Dover, gouging out with huge eroding force a trench. This washed away the land connection between southern Britain and northern France, thus leaving our islands much as they are today, completely separated from the continental mainland.

So we have safely rounded the southeastern corner of the British Isles and will head west along the English Channel in the next chapter to continue our journey around our shores.

TEN

—

A TALE OF SHIPPING
AREA TURBULENCE

PART TWO

Gathering speed, we rejoin our exploration of the sea areas, heading westwards along the English Channel.

WIGHT

—

The Wight sea area takes in a number of well-known places including Hastings, Brighton, Bognor Regis, Selsey, Chichester Harbour, Hayling Island, Portsmouth, the Isle of Wight itself and Southampton. This stretch of coastline has a rich naval history and now hosts a huge number of private craft.

Let's start at Chichester Harbour, which today holds thousands of privately-owned boats moored safely in its sheltered waters away from the open sea. The Romans headed straight in here in 43 AD for what turned out to be quite a long stay – 367 years, in fact – which actually was of great benefit to the whole area. During the Roman occupation, the rivers that ran into the sea were much deeper than they are today; over the subsequent centuries, many very large storms have affected the navigability of the rivers and the very use of some of the old harbours. Such has been the ferocity of the storms and the powerful tide sucking away at the fabric of the south coast, that land has vanished under the sea and then later reappeared. Chichester Harbour, for instance, has a very large sand bar almost right across its entrance, precluding all but shallow-draft boats from being able to come and go. The once-major ports of Steyning and Bramber are now high and dry, because of the silting up of the River Adur. Further downstream, the port of Old Shoreham, which goes back to the 11th century, is now useless as the river found another way out to sea at Portslade several miles to the east (which is where the New Shoreham port is now). I can vouch for the fact that the silt there is pretty dangerous. One summer when I was staying with my godmother in Shoreham, I went out with another boy along the shoreline. Almost immediately I sank into the mud up to my thighs. Somehow the other boy avoided my fate, but I needed to be rescued – and pretty damn fast too, as I was sinking still further. The stench was something best left undescribed! All I got for my pains was a severe telling-off from all and sundry, a hosing down to remove the offending stinking mud, and being told never to venture out there again on any account. I didn't.

Pagham Harbour has also alternated between being over and under water. Various attempts have been made to add sea defences, with some success. However, solving the problem in one place tends to move it along the coast to affect somewhere else, like Selsey for instance, where the encroachment of the sea becomes more obvious as each year goes by.

Newhaven is a place I remember from my teens. One dank chilly April morning I departed on a cross-channel ferry from there to Dieppe, a good four-hour journey. It was a school trip and we'd been looking forward to it for some time. However there was quite a storm brewing; we later learned that subsequent sailings that day were cancelled for safety reasons. Great. As we left the harbour, the waves crashed over the bows, and we began to wallow in a very disconcerting and sickening fashion. It was a bit of a baptism, having never put to sea before in my life. I was surrounded by hundreds of people, including fellow pupils with their contorted faces in various shades of green, or as white as the proverbial sheet, or very pale grey – all puking their guts up. I heaved a few times myself as we were tossed about like so much flotsam. I decided the best thing to do was to go and lie down somewhere, close my eyes and hope for the best. It worked, thank goodness, and never before or since have I been so glad to arrive somewhere. It was an extreme experience for a first sea journey, and I have been aboard various craft since then (usually in mill-pond conditions) – but good sailor, me? I think not. For getting from A to B in the shortest possible time (airport delays aside), I would rather fly any day of the week, thank you very much, and have mostly done just that ever since.

Further along the coast we have Southampton, and Southampton Water which is a tidal estuary just north of the Solent and the Isle of Wight. This area is most famous for its use by the yachting fraternity from the world over, and of course for the deep-water harbour that can accommodate the largest of ocean-going liners. Southampton's naval history stretches far back: it saw Henry V's army set sail for the Battle of Agincourt, the departure of the Pilgrim Fathers in the *Mayflower*, the departure of the *Titanic* on its fateful maiden and only voyage, and the despatch of the D-Day invasion fleet for Normandy. Not to be forgotten, though, is Henry VIII's favourite ship, the *Mary Rose*, which sailed in and out of Southampton's harbour. Reputedly named after Henry's sister Mary Tudor, the ship was built a few miles away in Portsmouth around the year 1510. The *Mary Rose's* last action was fighting a French invasion fleet in 1545, in what became known as the Battle of the Solent. Heavily laden with men and armaments, she was probably caught by a freak gust of wind that caused her to keel over, with water rushing in through the open lower gun ports. She capsized and sank very rapidly with a great loss of life; there were only about three dozen survivors out of a complement of at least 400 men. All this left Henry VIII with a heavy heart, witnessing from the shore the demise of his prize ship. The remains of the *Mary Rose*, which were salvaged from the bed of the Solent in 1982, are soon to be housed in a new purpose-built museum due for completion in 2012 at Portsmouth's Historic Dockyard.

So let's go to Portsmouth now, to glance at more of our naval history. Nelson's flagship at the Battle of Trafalgar, HMS *Victory*, is also on permanent display there, in Dry Dock No. 2, only a few yards from the Mary Rose museum. Incidentally the *Victory* has never been decommissioned, so is in fact the oldest commissioned naval ship in the world, and now has its 99th Commanding Officer, Lieutenant Commander Oscar Whild. Here too is where the Royal Yacht *Britannia*, used to call in for her annual refits, when she was still around and in use by the royal family. Portsmouth stands on the shore of a large natural harbour, whose use goes back as far as 400 BC when there was a dockyard in what is now Portchester. In the 3rd century AD the Romans built the fort of Portus Adurni overlooking the harbour. It was one of their Saxon shore forts, a series of coastal defences that protected this coast from Saxon raiders. Its walls, which were subsequently incorporated in medieval Portchester Castle, are now the best example of Roman walls in Northern Europe, still standing over seven metres high. Speeding through time, in the late 9th century King Alfred constructed his fleet in this general area, and with a further leap we come to the great shipbuilding era under Henry VIII, who is generally regarded as the founder of the Royal Navy. He added some 85 ships to the fleet in his reign, many of which were built at Portsmouth, including of course the *Mary Rose*. Much was to change in 1563 when 250 people died, many of them with hard-to-replace shipbuilding skills, in one of the town's periodic outbreaks of the plague. After a very quiet century for the dockyard, it was Oliver Cromwell who ordered some much-needed work to enlarge the docks, and much later, in 1864, the advent of steamships demanded further expansion. More recently still there had to be room for the gargantuan vessels of the 20th century, such as HMS *Dreadnought* and HMS *Queen Elizabeth*, and then later HMS *Intrepid*, the frigate HMS *Kent* and the aircraft carriers HMS *Hermes* and *Illustrious*.

And the word 'illustrious' well describes the 2,400-year history of these dockyards. They have seen huge changes to keep up with the alternative ways of construction required to be able to build and service the ever-larger and more complex giants of the sea wanted by an ever-changing clientele.

I mentioned in the previous chapter, record volumes of both large and small maritime traffic pass through the Dover Strait, and indeed the whole of the English Channel. Every now and again collisions take place, although nowhere near as often as you might think given the circumstances. When they do happen, they tend to grab the headlines. In mid-December 2002 a 50,000-tonne Norwegian-registered cargo ship heading from the Belgian port of Zeebrugge to Southampton, collided with a container ship in thick fog a few miles east of Ramsgate in the early hours of the morning and sank in about 90 minutes. The cargo was a collection of 2800 brand new BMWs, Saabs and Volvos, with a collective showroom value of about £70 million – ouch! Imagine filling out the insurance claim for that little lot, never mind the value of the ship. The next day a salvage operation was aborted because of bad weather. Because of damage from the salt water, the reported value of the cargo had now dropped in value to 'only' £30 million which was also nearer its 'factory gate' value before profits and taxes were added. A French warship was sent out from Cherbourg and stationed alongside to warn other shipping of the wreck hazard. Despite this, in the early hours of the following morning a 3000-tonne German cargo vessel collided with the submerged car carrier, which was lying in about a hundred feet of water, and became stuck. A representative of the Maritime and Coastguard Agency said that there was really no excuse for this second collision, as the two warning vessels that were now standing by were lit up like Christmas trees. Would you believe that a day later yet another collision with the sunken car carrier was narrowly averted? An alert coastguard aircraft spotted another ship heading directly for trouble, messages were sent and all was well, but it was a close call and the incident was registered as a 'near miss', with only about 400 yards to spare – not a lot when a big ship is altering course.

There was quite a bit of comment and gnashing of teeth at this ineptitude. An expert at the Seafarers International Research Centre came up with the worrying statistic that there were about 70 near misses a day, blamed on human error or just poor skills. Another expert, this time from the National Union of Marine Aviation and Shipping Transport Officers (a title and a half!), was even more outspoken. "Cost-cutting and inept crews," he said, "would mean that it was not a case of if, but when, a passenger ferry would be involved in a serious collision with the great risk of loss of life." All this reminded many people, particularly in Zeebrugge, of the awful disaster there in March 1987 involving a RORO (roll-on / roll-off) ferry named MS *Herald of Free Enterprise*, as it set off for Dover with 80 crew members, 459 passengers, 81 cars, 3 buses and 47 lorries onboard. To speed up departure in calm weather, it was quite normal for a RORO ferry to delay closing the hinged bow and stern embarkation doors until the ship had pulled away from the dock, as there were other safeguards to prevent unwanted water ingress. However, that day the crew member on the *Herald of Free Enterprise* whose job it was to shut the doors once the ship started moving was asleep, and there was no warning mechanism to tell the Captain on the bridge that the doors were still open as the ferry moved out of the harbour. This was not the only issue: the *Herald's* loading ramps did not naturally match up to those on Zeebrugge dock, so to allow the ferry to board two decks simultaneously, the forward ballast tanks were filled before loading. It was the combination of these factors and the speed of departure that led to water rushing through the open doors. The vessel became unstable and capsized, all within a minute. More through luck than anything else it sank in quite shallow water less than a mile from port. The death toll was still 193 people – the worst peacetime maritime disaster involving a British-registered ship since 1919. Many of those who died didn't drown but succumbed to hypothermia in the very cold water. The subsequent inquiry identified many failings in the design and operation of these ferries, which were later rectified so – it is hoped – such an event could never happen again.

Although we have been discussing the history of the sea area of Wight, the Isle of Wight doesn't feature directly in our naval history. Its inhabitants began fending off invaders from about 1900 BC; this continued right through the Roman invasion, and was later followed by attacks by the Danes and the French, who landed further north. However, there were no great naval battles, as the inhabitants tended to defend attacks from their shores, rather than sailing out to meet incoming invaders in the surrounding waters.

In the previous chapter I mentioned that in days gone by a cricket match was held at low tide one day a year on the Goodwin Sands off the Kent coast. Well, would you believe there was another such annual occasion, this time in the incredibly busy shipping lanes of the Solent, the stretch of water between the mainland and the Isle of Wight. The Brambles Sandbank lies slap bang in the middle of the Solent and is – to the uninitiated – something of a shipping hazard. There is a long list of ships that have run aground here, one of the more recent being the *QE2* on its final visit to Southampton before retiring.

PORTLAND

The Portland sea area takes its name from the tiny island, four miles long by a mile and a half wide, that lies just south of Weymouth in the English Channel and is connected to the mainland by the famous Chesil Beach. Portland Harbour is one of the biggest man-made harbours in the world. Right from the start it was a Royal Navy base. It had a military role in both world wars and remained prominent in the latter half of the 20th century, as the navies of the NATO-member countries performed naval exercises in those waters right up until 1995. Since then the port has been used exclusively for civilian use. Looking ahead to the 2012 Olympic Games, the Weymouth and Portland National Sailing Academy will be playing host to all the sailing events.

PLYMOUTH

We leave the Dorset coast behind us now and reach Devon and the Plymouth sea area, named of course after the town. Plymouth has a long and proud naval history, stretching back to around 700 BC when it was Britain's number-one port. Along the way, Hoe was the setting for a certain game of bowls that Sir Francis Drake was playing as the Spanish Armada advanced, if the stories are to be believed. The port was of utmost importance in the Napoleonic wars, providing huge support to both Nelson and the Duke of Wellington in their ultimately successful campaigns against Napoleon. What was once named Plymouth Dock became known as Devonport in 1824. By quite early in the 20th century, Devonport had become the most renowned naval port in the world. In World War I five of the 14 ships lost in the Battle of Jutland in the North Sea were based there. In World War II it harboured ships used in both the Battle of the Atlantic and the D-Day landings, but its docks were an obvious – indeed prime – target for German bombing raids, which did huge damage to both the port and large parts of the city. The next major phase of Devonport's history came in 1982 when many of the ships needed for the Falklands conflict were prepared and visited by the victuallers there, in readiness for the very long voyage down to the South Atlantic and then for the fight with the Argentine forces to recapture the Falkland Islands. More recently, nuclear submarine facilities have been built there and a Government contract granted for the servicing of Royal Navy vessels.

We can't leave this area without mentioning a catastrophic accident in March 1967 involving a supertanker named the *Torrey Canyon*. This ship, with a mind-blowing capacity of 120,000 tons, was en route from Kuwait to Milford Haven, when it took a shortcut. This put the ship on course to collide with a fishing fleet, and then there was confusion between the Master and the helmsman (who was also the ship's cook with little experience at the helm) about whether the ship was in manual or automatic steering mode. By the time this was sorted out, disaster was unavoidable: the ship struck the Severn Stones reef between the Cornish coast and the Scilly Isles. The rocks ruptured the oil tanks, causing a huge outflow of crude oil into the sea and thence onto both the Cornish and French coasts. A contamination problem on this scale had never happened in our waters before, and the action taken to deal with it was born more of desperation than of knowledge or planning. Royal Navy vessels pumped a vast amount of detergent into the sea in an attempt to disperse the oil. This, however, had little effect, and caused just as much damage to fish and sea birds as the oil itself. What followed, in an attempt to minimise the ensuing disaster, was extraordinary. The Government of the day, under Prime Minister Harold Wilson, ordered the Fleet Air Arm to set fire to the oil by dropping 42 1000-pound bombs on the stricken ship. The bombs repeatedly missed their target, and a quarter were in effect wasted. Next, the Air Force dropped cans of aviation fuel onto the oil in an attempt to burn it off. An almighty barrage of munitions was used, including in the end the use of Napalm, to set the oil alight. This was Britain's Operation Orange on the high seas. While much was learned from this shambles, it was not the finest hour for the British Government, the Navy or the Air Force. At the time it was the costliest maritime disaster to have happened anywhere.

On a lighter note, later that year, four young men – myself being one – were aboard a somewhat smaller vessel on the Norfolk Broads enjoying a week chugging to and fro from pub to pub and being stopped for speeding by the Broads Police on more than one occasion. The limit was five knots and as we had no way of measuring our speed, and were a bit worried about how much water the boat was taking on board because of a leaking prop-shaft flange, we were more concerned about getting to shallower water, in case the worst happened and we sank. One of us had had the novel idea – in the light of what had happened earlier in the year – of renaming our boat the *Torrey Canyon*, in very large letters fore and aft. (Its proper name was something boring like *Moonlit Waters* and he thought we should have something more topical-sounding.) This caused much merriment amongst fellow holiday boaters; the occupants of one boat were so amused by the name that they stopped looking where they were going and buried the prow of their boat several feet into the reeds on the bank. The renaming did cause a problem, though, when we had to navigate a lock, for which we had booked a time-slot. So busy was the lockkeeper looking for a boat called *Moonlit Waters* (which of course he didn't find) that we lost our slot; we were given a right royal wigging by said lockkeeper when the truth dawned. Happy days.

BISCAY
—

Heading south past the Brest Peninsula on France's west coast we enter the next sea area – that of the Bay of Biscay. During World War II, German U-boat men called this area the 'valley of death', because the RAF picked off and sank more than 70 U-boats in these waters. This area is renowned for its rough weather, caused in part by the continental shelf that juts out some miles under the sea, making it relatively shallow. Many ships have foundered here over the centuries with great loss of life. Greater knowledge, better-built ships and improvements in weather forecasting, including our friend the Shipping Forecast, have played their part in making traversing this sector of the ocean so much safer in recent years. Even still, there are times when the might of nature overcomes all of man's best efforts. One such occasion was in December 1999, when huge seas caused the *Erika* oil tanker to break up and sink. This time the crew were saved with the help of helicopters from both the French and British navies, preventing any loss of life. The financial penalties were high, though, with not only the loss of an expensive cargo of oil but also substantial fines for the damage caused by the leaked oil to the French habitat, including the loss of an estimated 300,000 seabirds.

The *Torrey Canyon* and the *Erika* are but two of many examples of the damage that can result from making all shipping larger. But the trend still continues, as shipbuilders try to accommodate the voracious appetite of the human race for more oil to be carried greater distances in less time, bigger container ships to shift more goods to more countries as cheaply as possible, and more and more people to be able to travel on passenger liners across the globe to explore the furthest reaches of our world. Many heads have sat round numerous tables the world over to reassess what should be done when one of these leviathans of the sea comes a cropper, and although in general answers have been found, each time something new goes wrong it does throw up the fact that sadly no two incidents are ever the same and it is very hard to legislate for all possibilities.

TRAFALGAR

We reach the southernmost point in our journey as we enter Trafalgar. This sea area takes its name from Cape Trafalgar, a headland in the province of Cadiz in south west Spain. It was off this headland in 1805 – during the Napoleonic Wars – that one of the most famous and decisive naval battles ever was fought, between the British ships (under the command of Admiral Lord Nelson) and the French and Spanish ships (under the French Admiral Pierre Villeneuve). The French and Spanish lost two-thirds of their ships and the British none. However, as we all know from our schooldays, Horatio Nelson was killed, felled by a single shot from a range of about 50 feet by a French sharpshooter high up in the rigging of the *Redoutable*. Nelson had earlier been warned that his distinctive uniform was inviting target practice from the opposing ships which were fighting at very close quarters, but he spurned the advice – and the rest, as they say, is history.

FITZROY

—

Now we start our journey north, which takes us up the west side of the UK. It brings us first of all to the FitzRoy sea area. As mentioned in some detail in Chapter Three, this name was chosen for the area in 2002, in recognition of Vice-Admiral Robert FitzRoy's founding of our Meteorological Office, as the previous name for this area – Finisterre – had to be changed to avoid confusion with the same name in the Spanish forecast area.

SOLE

—

There's not a great deal to say about the Sole sea area, except that it takes its name from a couple of sandbanks named Little Sole Bank and Great Sole Bank. In 1989 this was one of the many sea areas subject to Government restrictions for cod fishing, as there were fears that cod was being over-fished. The eponymous fish, sole, is prolific here – they prefer warmer waters and in this sea area they benefit from the Gulf Stream. However, they also appear in many other coastal waters round the UK too, the best known example of course being Dover sole.

LUNDY

—

And so to Lundy, named after Lundy Island in the Bristol Channel off the north Devon coast. This small island – its total area is about 1800 acres – has proved to be something of a hazard to shipping over the centuries, especially in fog. Countless vessels have collided with its inhospitable rocky cliffs, and divers have recovered all manner of items, the earliest being stone cannon-balls from the late 16th century. The *Jenny* sank here in 1797, and from time to time evidence comes to light of its cargo of ivory and gold dust. Another ship that placed itself firmly on Lundy's list of high-profile collisions was the HMS *Montagu*. In 1901 this three-year-old, million-pound pre-*Dreadnought* battleship was unwisely steaming at full speed in the fog and rammed Shutter Rock on the south west corner of the island, becoming firmly grounded. There were no casualties onboard, and a small party of sailors left the ship to get help. They thought they had hit the rocks on the mainland at Hartland Point and went to the lighthouse thinking it was the Hartland Point light. When they were told by the lighthouse keeper that they were not where they thought they were, a rather heated argument ensued. The keeper eventually won when he told the members of the crew in no uncertain terms that he knew which lighthouse he had been master of for some years. A shamefaced gaggle of naval crew members had to return to their stricken ship to report what they had discovered. The ship had impaled itself so firmly on the rocks that it had huge gashes in its hull below the water line; it had to be abandoned and later proved impossible to re-float or salvage, and was subsequently scrapped in situ. This was a navigational error of some 15 miles, which caused some extremely red faces back at the Admiralty.

A friend of mine, Bob Gilliat, used to be Agent for the Landmark Trust, which leases Lundy from its present owners, the National Trust. He tells the story of how this came about in the following way:

"I was intrigued to see a headline in the *Sunday Express* saying: 'Who is to be the next King of Lundy?' The article referred to an advertisement for a new Agent for Lundy Island. Out of curiosity, I applied for the job, along with 912 others, and to my surprise and with some misgivings, was appointed by the Landmark Trust. This organisation had, without doubt, saved the island for the nation when it came up for sale in 1968. Jack

Hayward, the Bahamian entrepreneur, had offered to buy it for the National Trust – but the Trust could not accept it as it was not endowed to do so. At the 11th hour the trustees of the Landmark Trust agreed to take a 60-year £1 lease on the island and guaranteed to carry out the extensive restoration of historic buildings required by the National Trust's rules so that they could accept ownership. Since 1968 the Landmark Trust has spent millions of pounds in restoring this magical island for the enjoyment of nature lovers and those who believe in nurturing the English heritage we have inherited from previous generations. I arrived in August 1978 on the regular supply vessel the *Polar Star*, and was landed by coble, the island's flat-bottomed high bowed fishing boat, to be greeted by the 28 islanders employed by the Landmark Trust to run the island. Many were skilled tradesmen who carried out the promised restoration work, some ran the farm and operated the boats, while others, including the wives (as every islander was expected to work) kept the island running and the holidaymakers happy. A very mixed crowd they were, although they had one thing in common – a love of Lundy. Running an island was in complete contrast to my previous life – 32 years in the Army and then working for a London civil engineering consultant – although without doubt a unique experience."

Bob Gilliat later told me that during his five-year stint on the island between 1978 and 1983 he became all too aware of the weather on a daily basis. Unless you were indoors, there was nowhere to hide if it was 'acting up'. When the weather was so bad that it jeopardised the safe arrival of the supply ship (which doubled as visitor transport from the mainland) he was faced with a difficult problem. He had to weigh up not only if it were safe enough for it to make landfall on the island but also, using information from the Shipping Forecast, whether it was going to be able to set sail again safely later in the day. A miscalculation could result in some 700 visitors being stranded on the island, with all kinds of resulting problems – especially where to accommodate and feed them. Some years after he left, this very situation occurred and 700 people had to stay on the island until 0200 the following morning. The only available accommodation was the church hall, and the pub ran out of food and beer. Embarrassment all round.

Bob was on Lundy during the ill-fated Fastnet Race of 1979 (more on that incident in the next sea area section). He tells the story of a small yacht with a family of four on board that had been knocked flat some 10 miles to the west of the island, and had taken on a lot of water in very high seas. Bob spotted the boat with binoculars and contacted a German container ship nearby, asking it to stand by and give lee protection. This it did until the stricken craft (using its engine as a storm jib) was opposite Rat Island. Just as the yacht was about to round up into the landing bay, its engine failed. In this urgent situation the island's coble was launched, which managed to get the yacht safely anchored and into shelter. The family, a Milford Haven architect and his wife and two small boys, stayed on the island until the storm abated. Bob recollects that his house was festooned with wet bedding and clothing for some days, until the family's yacht could be baled out and made ready for the open sea once more. There would have been no chance of getting a lifeboat to rescue this family, as all the local ones were already out helping the Fastnet yachts.

Finally, Bob tells me that Lundy has recently become the first Marine Conservation Area, having already been made the first marine nature reserve in the early 1980s.

FASTNET

So now we move to the Fastnet sea area, named after Fastnet Rock, the turning point in the world-famous yacht race that bears its name. The race is the climax of the Admiral's Cup competition. It takes place over a 608-mile course, starting at Cowes on the Isle of Wight, sailing westwards past Land's End and then north across the Irish Sea, rounding Fastnet Rock with its lighthouse, before returning south and ending at Plymouth. The winning time is usually between three and four days to complete the course. The race was first held in 1925, and was an annual event for the first seven years, since when it has taken place every other year (except during World War II). And so, we come as promised to the sad story of the 1979 Fastnet Race, which also brought the Shipping Forecast itself under the spotlight. On this particular occasion in August 1979, on the opening day of the race the competitors were worried by the seeming lack of wind they were going to encounter that day, plus the likely presence of some fog en route, although the Shipping Forecast that lunchtime indicated that there would be *'south westerly winds, four or five increasing to six to seven for a time'*. Two days later the wind was reported to be force six (strong breeze) with gusts to force seven (near gale), with further predictions that winds would reach force eight. However, in the event many yachts were caught in violent force 10 gusts when they were about halfway between Land's End and Fastnet. The Weather Centre, which was still based at Bracknell then, had been tracking this storm across the Atlantic for some time and working with the aid of computer models and information coming in from weather ships to measure its strength and direction over the period of the race. Everything appeared reasonable; the forecasters could see that the storm was not to be ignored, but it didn't give undue cause for concern. Although the cyclonic nature of this low-pressure weather system was quite likely to strengthen, there was no reason to believe that it would change as suddenly or to the extent that it did, bringing about the severity of the storm that followed and the tragedy that this caused. Part of the weather system became unstable, which was not detected – or perhaps was not even detectable – until it was too late. The ferocity of the winds, which by now were blowing in several different directions at once, whipped up the seas producing waves of up to 15 metres at times. It was more the effect of the wind on the sea, rather than the wind itself, which was to overwhelm so many craft.

What happened next was the worst disaster in the history of offshore racing. Fifteen crew members died and 24 yachts were lost or abandoned. The former Prime Minister, Edward Heath, was one of those reported missing, but he later made it back to shore unharmed. Many of those who were lost had fallen overboard as their safety harnesses snapped – although thankfully 136 sailors were rescued by dint of an amazing air/sea operation. Helicopters from RNAS *Culdrose* in Cornwall were scrambled and made countless sorties. Soon these Sea King helicopters were joined by others from RNAS *Yeovilton*. The Royal Navy frigate HMS *Broadsword* set sail from Plymouth to direct the rescue operations. An RAF Nimrod acted as a spotter plane, reporting back to the choppers and surface rescue ships any craft it spotted in distress. A Dutch warship and French trawlers also provided assistance. The upshot of this catastrophe included a drastic review of the Fastnet Race rules by the Royal Ocean Racing Club, after it had been cleared of blame for the disaster. The new rules included a limit of 300 yachts competing in the race, and the insistence that boats carry more ballast and that improvements be made to the webbing of safety harnesses, some of which had proved to be woefully wanting in strength. It was made mandatory for all vessels to carry VHF radio equipment and for all competitors to hold valid sailing qualifications. Four years later the previous restrictions on the use of electronic navigational aids were also lifted. The information that was broadcast by the BBC in the Shipping Forecast on the day the race started, and the following forecasts, came under critical review. However, the BBC pointed out that it was purely the instrument of broadcast of the information presented to them by the forecasters at the Central Forecasting Office at Bracknell. That was always the case and remains so to this day.

The race has continued to be held every other year, without further serious incident, with the above-mentioned improvements in place. Boats are better constructed now, 30-odd years on, and thankfully there has been no repeat of those extreme weather conditions, although it is never a doddle in these waters.

IRISH SEA

After that tale of woe, we arrive at the Irish Sea, named after this bit of briny. You may well have crossed it if you have ever headed for Ireland on one of the many ferry services, with or without your car. The only other way across is to fly, as there is no road bridge and no tunnel. There has been talk, in fact, about building a rail-only tunnel for over a hundred years now, on the same lines as the Chunnel under the English Channel. Four possible routes have been earmarked and the technical problems are apparently not insurmountable. However (and there is always a *however* on these occasions) the project is not seen as economically viable despite the quite high volume of traffic that traverses the sea. In other words don't hold your breath: the likelihood of this happening any time soon, if at all, is remote. The experience from the Chunnel has not helped the case for an Irish Sea tunnel, because the passenger numbers using the Chunnel have never matched the estimated numbers used to justify its construction. The projected time of construction and the cost for an Irish Sea tunnel (bearing in mind that the Chunnel ended up costing almost double the projected sum of £5.2 billion) are further large hurdles to overcome. As you can imagine, the airlines and ferry companies would not exactly fall over themselves in lending support to this project either.

In the meantime, ships are the main way of moving vehicles and especially goods, between Ireland and Britain or beyond. Although the weather can of course cause delays to shipping, everything seems to work pretty well. It is pretty busy too, with the transit of over 30 million tons of cargo each year out of Liverpool, some 10 million tons of goods traded from Northern Ireland to Britain, and 7.5 million tons out of the various ports in the Irish Republic. In addition to all that, about four million passengers go to and fro each year.

In the latter stages of World War I, after the USA had entered the conflict in 1917, the Irish Sea became known as *U-boat Alley*, as the German submarines left the Atlantic and found considerably easier pickings here.

SHANNON

—

We move over to the other side of Ireland now and look out over the full force of the Atlantic Ocean which brings in so much of our weather. The next stop in that direction is the USA, but that's not where we will be going at all. We are currently passing lovely County Clare and the River Shannon, the longest in Ireland, which lends its name to the sea area. No fewer than nine ships have also been named after the river, between the years 1757 and 1875. One in particular, HMS *Shannon* built in 1806, fought in the Napoleonic Wars and, in 1813, fought and captured the American frigate USS *Chesapeake*. She then had an island named after her – Shannon, off Greenland.

ROCKALL

—

Still firmly in the Atlantic we move up to Rockall. On one occasion when I asked a colleague whether any of the pages of the Shipping Forecast were in yet (as it was rather close to transmission time), he replied succinctly, after looking forlornly at the telex machine, "Sorry to say, 'Rock-all'."

So what is Rockall? It's a fairly small rock jutting out of the North Atlantic, the tip of the eroded core of an extinct volcano, and home to gannets, seagulls and periwinkles. When I say small, it really is – 19 metres high by 25 across and 30 wide – so the afore-mentioned wildlife have to get on pretty well with each other. Considering its insignificant size, it seems amazing that there have been two major shipwrecks on it, the second of which was the more serious, when the SS *Norge* foundered in 1904, killing around 600 people. It's also amazing, on the face of it, that the UK, Ireland, Iceland and even Denmark have for years been arguing their socks off over the territorial rights to this lump of granite quartz rock poking out of the ocean and covered in bird droppings. Ah, but it's not the rock itself they are interested in, it's what it sits on – the Rockall Bank, which some geologists believe contains a very substantial amount of natural gas and oil, a potentially lucrative prize indeed.

There is also the matter of the very plentiful fish stocks to be harvested around it. The matter has not yet been resolved. In fact, according to John Vidal, writing in *The Guardian* on January 1st, 2011, the UN is investigating and will decide which nation has legal possession of Rockall by 2012. In the meantime, we can expect that the activist charity Greenpeace will attempt to claim the rock as theirs again, as happened in June 1997, when John Vidal and others landed on the rock. Greenpeace later managed to put up a plaque on Rockall that read: '*Let the sun and wind do their work. Leave the oil beneath the waves.'* This plaque has by all accounts now disappeared, although I am not sure many of us will be able to climb onto the venerable rock to check whether it is still in place.

There have been reports in national newspapers that there are two unexploded World War II bombs near the rock, but it's probably safer to leave them there than to try to fish them out. If they ever went off, the local fauna would have a hell of a fright and a nasty headache. Needless to say this strange little rock gives its name to the sea area.

MALIN

We have about half a dozen areas to go in our saga of the shipping areas around the shores of the British Isles. We have now reached Malin, which is by Malin Head, the most northerly headland on the Irish mainland. It had its own moment of importance during World War II, when the Irish Government allowed the British to put two radio direction finders there in a top secret operation to monitor U-boats and other activities in the North Atlantic.

If you are in any way an ornithologist you would want to visit Malin Head to catch sight of the hard-to-come-by corncrake and, in the autumn, to witness the migration south of gannets, shearwaters, skuas, auks and many other seabirds.

Across the water on the eastern side of this sea area we reach the west coast of Scotland, where we find HM Naval Base Clyde, one of the three bases in the UK for the Royal Navy, and the only one in Scotland. (The other two are HMNB Devonport and HMNB Portsmouth, both on the south coast of England.) Clyde is home to the UK's strategic nuclear deterrent of submarines armed with

Trident missiles. The submarine base is about 25 miles west of Glasgow and comprises several sites; the two main ones are RNAD Coulport, the armaments depot, and Faslane. In late 2010 Clyde saw the arrival of HMS *Astute*, the first in her class of anti-submarine and anti-surface-warfare submarines, that had just completed a year of trials. This is a very self-reliant class of craft, which I fancy will not need to be very interested in the Shipping Forecast – among other things. It submerges for three months at a time, only having to come up for air as it were, to restock its copious food stores and freezers to feed its 98-man crew. It is nuclear-powered, so has no need of re-fuelling for its projected 25 years of operational life. It creates its own water and air supply, and has such sophisticated electronics that it no longer requires a periscope that has to be raised and lowered through its hull. Instead it has other means of being able to see what is around it, both above and below water, with incredibly high resolution cameras plus thermal imaging and – well you name it. It has also been coated with nearly 40,000 acoustic panels on the outside. These make it the equivalent of the *stealth bomber* – undetectable by other ships, as these panels mask its sonar signature. In theory, and I'm sure in practice too, an enemy submarine or surface ship or indeed land-based target could fall prey to the substantial firepower of this state-of-the-art war machine before knowing what had happened. It is, in popular parlance, *truly awesome*. It will be joined before long by two others in this class, HMS *Ambush* and HMS *Artful*. These subs have been built at the BAE Systems shipyard in Barrow-in-Furness, Cumbria.

HEBRIDES

—

We remain in the Atlantic as we come next to Hebrides, named after the group of islands off the north west of Scotland including Lewis, Harris, North Uist, Benbecula, South Uist and Barra. The climate up here is remarkably constant for such a northerly outpost, but this is in part as a result of the influence of the Gulf Stream, which passes close by, with its associated warm air and water. Lying on the west of the British Isles and subject to the vagaries of North Atlantic storms, the islands have caused a few maritime disasters by getting in the way of shipping, with a catalogue of wrecks still to be found in these waters. Because of the danger, there are no less than three lighthouses to aid safe navigation. Still, though, the worst has happened: in 1853, 350 out of the 450 people on board the *Annie Jane*, an immigrant ship bound from Liverpool to Montreal, lost their lives when the ship foundered on the rocks at Vatersay.

The route into Stornaway Harbour on Lewis has always been (and still is) difficult to navigate. In the early hours of New Year's Day in 1919 the *Iolaire*, which had left the port of Kyle of Lochalsh the evening before heavily laden with sailors returning home after World War I, hit some notorious rocks called 'The Beasts of Holm' just a few yards out from the shore and only a mile or so from the entrance to Stornoway Harbour. The men were in full naval uniform, including very heavy footwear that made 'swimming for it' all but impossible for any but the very fittest. There were about 300 on board at the time of this accident, but only 75 survived. This was the worst maritime disaster – in terms of numbers killed – in UK waters in peacetime since the wrecking of the SS *Norge* off Rockall in 1904, and the worst peacetime disaster to involve a British ship since the loss of the *Titanic* in 1912. A gloomy distinction, to be sure.

BAILEY

—

Sea area BAILEY is something of an odd man when it comes to providing a definitive answer as to why this area of sea water is called what it is called. As someone once said 'there's always one' and on this occasion, Bailey is it. All I know for certain is that it is named after a sand bank – as indeed are other sea areas that we have talked about – and lies between Scotland and Iceland. It was originally part of 'The Western Area' before this specific part of the sea area became *Bailey*, named after said sand bank in 1949. If Bailey had been the outermost wall of a castle, or the photographer David or a pre-fabricated bridge, there would have been so much more to tell. Sea area Bailey alas is the proverbial mystery wrapped in a North Atlantic enigma of sea spray. There is no more to say about it. It's there, but is purely a mass of water between sea areas Rockall and South East Iceland. Very frustrating.

FAIR ISLE

Next, as we approach the finish line is the Fair Isle sea area, named after an island that is described as Britain's most remote (though far from isolated) inhabited island. Most of us associate the name with those splendid, warm and instantly recognisable sweaters that the women of the island make, while their men folk are engaged in crofting. Like so many northern islands, birds are plentiful, making it a great destination for those interested in seeking them out, armed with binoculars of course. Wind turbines have provided the inhabitants' power needs for about the last 20 years. For those interested in World War II relics, there are the remains of an RAF radar station and the recognisable chunks of a Heinkel that crashed during the war.

FAEROES

The Faeroes sea area is named after the group of islands that have been under the control of Denmark since 1380. The two different spellings – Faeroes and Faroes – are both correct, so you can take your pick. The islands lie about halfway between Great Britain and Greenland. In 1940 they were occupied by British troops, following the occupation of Denmark by Nazi Germany. This was to protect and strengthen control over shipping movements in the North Atlantic. The main concern, as mentioned earlier, was the protection of Allied merchant shipping convoys bringing vital supplies from America and the South Atlantic to Britain and the Soviet Union. Britain was heavily reliant upon these supplies, which could amount to over a million tons per week, to continue its war effort against the Germans. However, the German U-boats and warships were taking a heavy toll on these convoys. The struggle continued throughout the war years, from 1939 to 1945. After the war, control of the Faeroe Islands was once more restored to Denmark.

In 2010 there was the making of a repeat of the Cod Wars between Iceland and Great Britain, although this time the fish concerned was the mackerel. The Faeroes had tripled its usual fishing entitlement, which led to Scottish fishermen blockading a Faeroese trawler from landing its catch (valued at £400,000). So another row over fishing quotas is once again rearing its ugly head in the northern waters.

Nearby lie the Orkney Islands and a site which was writ large in both world wars: Scapa Flow. The British used it as a northern base for their naval activities. Prior to World War I, all of the chief naval bases had been in the English Channel to fight off the traditional foes from France, Spain and the Netherlands. However, in World War I the German navy began building warships like there was no tomorrow, and these would set sail from the Baltic heading for either the North Atlantic or down into the North Sea. When this building programme was detected, the realisation dawned that our naval forces would be put to better use off the northernmost reaches of the UK, to keep an eye on what was emerging from the direction of the Baltic Sea. Although Scapa Flow was not fortified, it was decided that the British Grand Fleet should be stationed there. There were attacks from U-boats, but minefields, artillery batteries and concrete barriers were installed and, with the aid of the newly-invented hydrophones to listen out for enemy submarines, the whole place was made much more secure. When the Germans were defeated the whole of their fleet was impounded in Scapa Flow while the future Versailles Peace Treaty was being hammered out. The British ships left on exercises and the German Officer in Command of the impounded fleet gave the order for the entire fleet to be scuttled so that the vessels would not fall into British hands. Some 51 of the 78 ships impounded were sunk, without loss of life.

In World War II a German U-boat succeeded in penetrating the Scapa Flow defences and torpedoed HMS *Royal Oak*, which quickly capsized with the loss of over 800 of its 1400 crew members. The wartime Prime Minister Winston Churchill ordered that further protective measures should be implemented to stop this kind of attack happening again.

Scapa Flow has had a completely different purpose since drilling for North Sea oil started in the early 1970s. A terminal was built there to receive and process the oil fed in by pipeline from the Piper Oil Field (mentioned in the previous chapter in the FORTIES section). Oil is still piped in to the terminal, now coming from the Claymore and Tartan oil fields.

SOUTH EAST ICELAND

—

Iceland, and the waters between it and the Faeroes, have seen much activity in both the world wars, as well as the Cod Wars and (as just mentioned in the FAEROES section) perhaps soon could again in something that has already been dubbed the Mackerel Wars but which it is hoped will not come to fruition.

Iceland is seismically active as manifested frequently one way or another. In just the last decade there were two earthquakes recorded in 2000 and another in 2008, followed of course by the volcanic activity in 2010 that sent the notorious ash clouds billowing out of the Eyjafjallajökull volcano. This caused huge disruption to international flights and considerable damage to Iceland's domestic economy. However it is the sea-based stories that we are most interested in as we reach the final sea area covered by the Shipping Forecast.

Let's have a look at the Cod Wars, or, to give them their full name, the Icelandic Cod Wars. For centuries Iceland's economy has been almost entirely dependent upon the millions of tons of fish it has harvested from its waters. When boats became more mechanised, it was possible to go further and further afield in search of even larger catches. Back in 1893 Denmark, which governed both Iceland and the Faeroe Islands at that time, decided to impose a 13-nautical-mile fishing limit around their shores; British trawlers didn't recognise this limit and continued to fish in these disputed waters, with the result that Danish gunboats, intent on upholding their law, escorted many of the British trawlers to their ports, fined them and also confiscated their catches. The British point of view was: if one North Sea nation decided to impose such limits, there was nothing to prevent others from following suit, and strangling the British fishing industry. There were many incidents, including

British trawlers being fired upon and actual damage being caused. At no time was the Royal Navy brought in to defend these unarmed trawlers from the assault on them. The outbreak of World War I brought the whole thing to a halt, as it became too dangerous for any serious fishing activities to take place here.

The territorial issue remained unresolved for many years, and in 1958 Iceland (now independent of Denmark) decided to up the stakes and increase the small *no fish zone* around its shores from four to twelve nautical miles. As this restriction on British trawlers' 'rights' was still unrecognised by the British Government, this time our trawlers sought its protection and got its permission to continue fishing in these waters guarded by naval warships. This was all well and good, but it cost the British Government a fortune in manning and fuelling all these naval ships to carry out these protection duties. Many incidents occurred in which shots were fired, and some damage was sustained, but at least nobody was hurt. This 'first' Cod War ended with both sides agreeing that any further disputes should go before the International Court of Justice at The Hague.

In 1972 Iceland extended her fishing limits to 50 nautical miles. This time not only British trawlers, but also German ones, ignored the regulation and continued to fish within these limits, against the Icelanders' wishes and from their point of view breaking the law. Matters deteriorated in this Second Cod War when Iceland threatened to leave NATO, as she felt NATO had done nothing to help sort out this dispute; Britain was also a NATO member of course. We were still in the Cold War at this point, remember, and NATO's dilemma was that it was using various ports in Iceland as bases for warships guarding the Greenland-Iceland-UK-Gap, principally from Soviet submarines. In November 1973 a deal was struck, but that expired two years later – and tensions escalated again as Iceland laid claim now to a 200-mile exclusion zone.

In this Third Cod War Icelandic boats used net cutters against the British trawlers as they had done in the earlier conflict. There were many incidents also involving collisions, gunfire and damage, all coming to a head when Iceland threatened to close down the NATO base at Keflavík on its west coast. The military defence thinking at the time viewed this with dismay in view of the perceived threat from the Soviet Union. The British Government backed down and the Icelandic claim to a 200-mile exclusion zone was effectively conceded even though no specific agreement was made. The result of all this brouhaha was that the British fishing industry, which was already in decline, was further damaged, causing some hardship in this country's major fishing ports of Grimsby, Hull and Fleetwood.

Much more recently, in 2010, thoughts went back to these events in the 1970s, when question marks were raised about the state of the mackerel fish stocks in the North Atlantic. Back in the seventies, oily fish such as mackerel were not at all popular, but tastes have changed so they are now in far greater demand. Both Iceland and the Faeroe Islands fish them extensively (within prescribed limits), although it seems the Faeroese have tripled their catch since 2007. This has brought about accusations of over-fishing, which came to a head in 2010 when a Faeroese trawler docking at Peterhead in Scotland was blockaded and refused permission to offload its £400,000 cargo. The agreed quotas are based on advice from the International Council for the Exploration of the Sea (ICES), whose most recent report states that since 2007 quotas had been exceeded by some 200,000 tons. The concern is that, at this rate, stocks would be exhausted by 2012 – cause for concern indeed on several levels. It's a case of 'watch this space.'

To end this tempestuous visit to South East Iceland I would like to broaden that area slightly to relate the following tale. Robert Terence Grogan was born in September 1899, raced motorbikes at the Brooklands race track near Weybridge in Surrey in the 1920s and later joined the Royal Navy. He was to die violently and suddenly on May 24th, 1941. Why do I mention him? Well, if he had lived four years longer he would have been my uncle. (Maybe you'll say he still counts as my uncle.) Anyway, what relevance does he have to this subject? I will tell you.

Terry Grogan had a penchant for working on engines and making them go faster. When he started racing Norton motorbikes, the size of the engines he sat astride then was in the region of 500cc. Later in World War II Terry was Commander (E) – the E meaning Engineering – on HMS *Hood*, which had been built in the John Brown shipyards on Clydebank between 1916 and 1918. The engines on *Hood* were a smidgen larger than Terry's motorbike, with an output of something like 144,000 shaft horsepower (a measure of the power from the boilers to the propeller shafts), equivalent to 107,000kW. After all, they had to move 47,500 tons of ship, munitions and men through the sea at over 30 miles per hour. *Hood* had had a complete overhaul and refit at the start of the war, but Terry still wanted more oomph from her engines. He knew what needed to be done and had at his disposal those who knew how to do it – by all accounts he succeeded.

When World War II was declared in September 1939, *Hood* was patrolling the waters around Iceland to protect merchant convoys from the German Navy. Her next job was to take part in the destruction of the French fleet to deny these vessels to the Germans. She was then sent to Scapa Flow to work on convoy escort duty, and to be in a good position to challenge any enemy shipping entering the North Sea or the Atlantic from the Baltic Sea. One of the most feared and ominously formidable German warships was the *Bismarck*, which in May 1941 was heading for the North Atlantic with the aim of attacking more convoys. The *Hood*, *Prince of Wales* and others were ordered to chase and intercept. The *Bismarck's* route took her far north and round the west coast of Iceland. The British ships took a fairly straight course out of Scapa Flow past the coast of south east Iceland, for an interception in the Denmark Strait, the strip of water between Iceland and Greenland. And so the encounter that followed became known as the Battle of Denmark Strait. It was short, sharp and brutal. *Hood* was hit by a lucky shell (from the Germans' point of view, highly unlucky from ours), which landed on her boat deck amongst some ready-to-use ammunition, causing a fire and several explosions. Shortly afterwards she was hit by another 15-inch shell from a range of about 10 miles, which hit and exploded the aft magazine. Such was the devastating force of this explosion that *Hood* broke in two and sank within three minutes, with the loss of all but three of her 1418 – man crew. The last of those three survivors died in 2010, but sadly Commander Robert Terence Grogan RN was not one of them – he died with the rest of *Hood's* crew in 1941. Terry had planned to join the BBC when the war ended. One of his hobbies was making recordings on 78rpm discs, some of which I still possess. It's consoling to think that all those years later I went on to do some of the things in the BBC that he had wanted to do.

Going back in time to 1912, it was at a point just a few hundred miles south of the location where HMS *Hood* was lost that the *Titanic* sank, with almost as high a death toll. In both cases the cold sea at these northern latitudes caused rapid hypothermia, killing many of those who had not already drowned.

Recently I met Admiral Sir Michael Layard, who had been very much involved in one particular refit at Devonport Naval Dockyard in preparation for the Falklands conflict. He was tasked with converting the *Cunard Atlantic Conveyor*, a RORO container ship that had been laid up in Liverpool, into a fully operational aircraft carrier, or Harrier Carrier as it was nicknamed – in an unbelievable nine days. The ship was moved from Liverpool down to Devonport. Instead of a crew of just 35, it now had to accommodate 125 with all basic amenities including fresh water, food and ablutions. The intention had been to take 650 men, but there simply was not room with everything else that had to be stowed aboard. (The remaining 500 men were taken to the South Atlantic by another RORO ferry, the *Norland*.)

Two flight decks were constructed on the *Atlantic Conveyor*, and the ship had to carry aviation fuel for its aircraft – these being eight Sea Harriers, six Harrier GR3s, five Chinook and six Wessex Helicopters – plus of course spare parts and ammunition. Stacking the aircraft on deck was a feat in itself. They all had to be wrapped in huge polythene bags to protect them from the elements in the 8000-mile voyage ahead, and fastened securely to the deck with special clamps, which had to be welded for the job. The rotor blades were removed from the helicopters, and more bags employed for them and the choppers themselves. The ship had to be fitted with the capability of re-fuelling whilst in transit, and all manner of other heavy engineering work had to be completed in an amazingly short time. An immense amount of stores had to be loaded carefully on board, bearing in mind what was likely to be needed to be offloaded first at the other end. A huge supply effort kicked into place, with lorry-loads and train-loads of provisions and ammunition flowing into the dockyard.

On April 25th, 1982, just nine days after arriving in Devonport, the *Atlantic Conveyor* began its long voyage south. There were sighs of relief and exhaustion from all at the dockyard as they watched the newly fitted-out *Atlantic Conveyor* sail away, knowing that an amazing job had been completed on time. One month later to the day, having arrived intact, she was hit by two Exocet missiles fired by two Super Etendard attack aircraft belonging to the Argentine airforce. The Exocets ripped through the port side a few feet above the water line – just above where the aviation fuel, munitions and general stores were housed. A fire was already raging. It took barely 20 minutes to realise that the ship was doomed, and would have to be abandoned before it would blow up and sink. An orderly evacuation took place with two other ships, *Alacrity* and *Sir Percival*, standing by to take aboard the *Atlantic Conveyor's* crew. Several helicopters were also involved in the rescue and saved five crew members from the burning and stricken *Conveyor*. It took about two and a half hours to scoop up all the survivors. During this time, though, the ship's Master, Ian North, was lost, believed drowned, along with 11 others. He and Michael Layard had worked in tandem on the epic refit of the *Conveyor*. Ian was the Master of the vessel, and Michael was the Senior Naval Officer. The two men had formed a friendship and deep respect for each other. As Michael recalls: "Many features have stuck in my mind, but two have left an indelible mark. Firstly, how brilliant the people were, in thought, strength of character and deed. Secondly, given willing hearts and when the need is imperative, there is no limit to what can be achieved. We astonished ourselves."

Now at last we have completed our long journey round the British Isles, taking in a chunk of history on the way. Time to move on and try and throw some light on some other aspects of this voyage of discovery.

ELEVEN

—

SHEDDING SOME LIGHT...
ON LIGHTHOUSES

Lighthouses around the coasts of the British Isles play an important part in ensuring the safety of those at sea, passing by our shores as they attempt to make safe landfall in harbours. This has been the case since the Romans constructed lighthouses on our shores in the 1st century AD. I've touched on a couple of lighthouse stories already, but now we look back into their history, to see who designed and built them and who manages them, with the odd spooky and strange story dropped in for good measure. Oh, and if you have ever wanted to live in one, they appear on the open market from time to time if you care to look on the right Internet sites. I dare say most of us would like to live in a light house, but how about a lighthouse? Certainly something a bit different to show off to your friends.

First of all let's take a look at the people who are in charge of these luminescent edifices dotted around our coasts and headlands. Three authorities work closely together to serve and protect all shipping round the British Isles. The Corporation of Trinity House, based in London, is the official General Lighthouse Authority for England and Wales and various other stretches of territorial waters including Gibraltar (but excluding Scotland, the Isle of Man and Northern Ireland). It is responsible for the maintenance of all navigational aids, including lighthouses, light vessels and buoys, plus in these days of advanced technology, all maritime radio and satellite communication systems. (As though that were not enough, Trinity House is also the Deep Sea Pilotage Authority, which supplies expert navigators for shipping trading in northern European waters.) The Northern Lighthouse Board has authority for the waters around Scotland and the Isle of Man and is responsible for the upkeep and maintenance of all lights, buoys and beacons in those areas. Lastly, the Commissioners of Irish Lights have very similar responsibilities for their jurisdiction of the whole of Ireland.

Trinity House was set up in the 12th century no less. The first written record shows that it was granted a Royal Charter by Henry VIII in 1514, a few hundred years later, as an organisation to better the welfare of seafarers around the coasts of 15th century England. Henry's daughter Elizabeth I granted a Coat of Arms to Trinity House in 1573 and in 1604 James I gave the organisation the right to the compulsory pilotage of shipping and also the exclusive licensing of pilots in the River Thames. It built its first lighthouse in 1609 at Lowestoft, financed by a levy of dues from shipping using the ports of Newcastle, Hull, Boston and King's Lynn. Much the same system of levies is still in use today. Many lighthouses were originally privately owned and financed, but reliability became something of an issue. The result was the compulsory purchase of all private lighthouses in England, Scotland, Wales and the Channel Islands. Under legislation passed in 1836, the private owners were compensated for their loss of revenue and other disbursements, and all the English and Welsh lighthouses were placed under the stewardship of Trinity House, which today looks after a total of 69.

All of these lighthouses are now automated, with the last one to be converted – in 1998 – being North Foreland in Kent. Although one thinks of automation as a very recent phenomenon, very clever use was made of a device dating from a hundred years ago. This 1910 invention, installed in several of the acetylene gas-powered lighthouses, relied on the rising sun to heat a black metal rod that was suspended vertically over and connected to the gas supply. As the rod heated up it expanded and switched off the gas during the daylight hours. The reverse happened when the sun went down, so the light came back on for the duration of the night. Clever stuff, and all before the widespread availability of the newfangled electric power. However, some lighthouses were oil-powered (or very early ones used wood or coal) so these had to be permanently manned in order to provide the warning beacons as reliably as possible 365 days a year. The early lighthouses were a bit hit or miss in their effectiveness. Full automation, as we understand it today, didn't begin until the early 1980s. Some of the more remote lighthouses have since had helipads installed onsite, to facilitate urgent access in the event of a failure. The rapid development of remote control technology now enables Trinity House to monitor all the lighthouses and lightships from its central planning unit in Harwich in Essex.

So what are the modern challenges facing Trinity House (and the other two General Lighthouse Authority (GLA) organisations that monitor and maintain these complex services round our coasts)?

The maritime traffic around our shores varies hugely, from the smallest single-man craft to enormous tankers and ever-larger passenger liners that need several miles to change course significantly, let alone stop. To aid their safe passage, Trinity House employs some 600 aids to navigation including lighthouses and sat nav systems. It also has to inspect and audit some 10,000 navigation items provided by local port and harbour authorities, as well as such remote structures as oil production platforms and, more recently, wind farms. There is also the small matter of locating any wrecks that could be a hazard to other shipping, placing warning beacons around them, and organising their removal where possible.

The increased use of sat nav has made everyone's job much easier and safer. The Marine Differential Global Positioning System (DGPS) uses a mix of visual, audible and electronic aids common to all three GLAs, with 14 ground-based DGPS networks providing coverage for a distance of about 50 nautical miles out from our shores and those of the Republic of Ireland. It is a system available to all, financed from the dues mentioned earlier.

In 2004 the GLA looked ahead to 2020 and published predictions of what would be required for marine navigation aids. The view was that lighthouses would remain an integral part of the plans for the foreseeable future.

So, how many lighthouses are there in the UK? By my reckoning there are about 150 working lighthouses altogether around the whole of the British Isles (the UK and the Republic of Ireland). Added to this are 27 no longer in use, and one listed as 'disused'. There are, however, several in Ireland that are neither listed as working nor as not working, which is a bit confusing – but at least we have a rough idea from these figures that there are a fair number altogether.

Before we talk about our own lighthouses we have to mention the Daddy of them all, the Pharos Lighthouse in Alexandria, Egypt, which was one of the Seven Wonders of the Ancient World. (The word *pharos* means 'lighthouse' in a number of languages.) The Pharos of Alexandria was huge. We will never be sure now exactly how large it was, but indications are that it was between 115 and 130 metres high, one of the tallest man-made structures for a very long time. As we mentioned in the DOVER section of Chapter Nine, the Romans built a lighthouse in Dubris (Dover) not that long after the Roman Conquest, and its tower still remains to this day in the grounds of the castle there.

British lighthouses can't compete for size with the Pharos of Alexandria, but we do have one or two notable ones to talk about. The Bell Rock Lighthouse, erected off Scotland's east coast and now 200 years old and counting, was originally known as Stevenson's Lighthouse – but was this correct? Robert Stevenson, who laid claim to its design, had based his plans on the famous Eddystone Lighthouse off the Cornish coast (which we will return to shortly). One John Rennie, however, claimed that it was he who had designed Bell Rock. So, whodunit? In 1799 Stevenson submitted some bold – and what were considered very expensive – plans to the Northern Lighthouse Board (NLB), which they rejected. Shortly thereafter in 1804 there was another tragedy as the HMS *York* ripped herself apart on the rocks, with the loss of almost 500 crew. Time for the NLB to think again urgently. John Rennie was asked to submit his ideas for the project before there were any more disasters. Eventually the NLB decided that both Rennie and Stevenson should work on the lighthouse, with Rennie as chief engineer and Stevenson his resident engineer. They agreed that their design should follow the Eddystone. So in 1807 Rennie returned to his comfy office in London to look after his lucrative practice there, while Stevenson with his large party of labourers and artisans struggled on in the most appalling conditions. Work was only possible during the summer months, for a couple of hours at each low tide. Needless to say, progress was slow and the deprivations great. In 1809, after two years' work, the tower was only a couple of metres high. Rennie made only a couple of visits to the construction site during the whole long process. However, he did contribute to the project, albeit from a distance. The lighthouse was at last completed in 1811. Even if there were ongoing arguments as to who had designed it, the Bell Rock Lighthouse was most assuredly built by Stevenson over a tortuous four-year period. Some said that in the end it looked more like his design than Rennie's.

There is an interesting postscript that centres around Stevenson's death in 1850 when the NLB made this announcement at a meeting (I quote from the minutes): *"The Board, before proceeding to business, desire to record their regret at the death of this zealous, faithful and able officer, to whom is due the honour of conceiving and executing the great work of the Bell Rock Lighthouse..."*

There was no doubt about how carefully these words were chosen, as present among those at the meeting were Stevenson's three sons David, Alan and Thomas. The sons were by then also in the family business of building lighthouses, part of the burgeoning and hugely accomplished Stevenson engineering dynasty. Those carefully chosen words read out at the meeting may sound cynical and may indeed have been a cynical ploy at the time, but one can follow the train of thought of whoever it was that wrote them. The Stevenson family – namely Robert, his sons David, Alan and Thomas, and in the third generation David's two sons David Alan and Charles – were to make lighthouse building in Scotland their life's work. Thomas's son was later to become famous in another sphere – as Robert Louis Stevenson, author of *Treasure Island*.

Before we move on to more lighthouses let's take a brief canter through the component parts of a traditional lighthouse so we understand more about the design. First there is the tower itself. Then at the top we have the lantern room, provided with supporting bars for the glass, to withstand the impact of high seas, plus stormproof ventilation to remove the considerable heat generated by the lantern – and in earlier times from the smoke created if oil-fuelled lamps were used. There is always a lightning rod, for obvious reasons. Underneath this area there is a watch-cum-service room to hold food and fuel supplies. There is often an outside balcony round the base of the lantern room – no, not for sunbathing, although I'm sure this must have been possible in better weather – but for cleaning the outside of the windows, which would constantly become caked with salt, cutting down the intensity of the beams. Some lighthouses had the luxury of separate keepers' quarters, a fuel store, a boat house and whatever else was deemed needed, depending on the location and the budget and the nature of the terrain for erecting buildings of any sort.

In the tale of the construction of the Bell Rock Lighthouse we mentioned the Eddystone Lighthouse, so let's go there next. As this lighthouse was constructed out at sea, on a pile of treacherous rocks 13 miles off the Cornish coast south west of Plymouth, the design had to contain everything within the tower. The first lighthouse was built in 1698 by Henry Winstanley. A merchant by trade, Winstanley decided to take the bull by the horns when the second of five ships he had invested in came to grief on the Eddystone Rocks. His first tower was built, with more than a little difficulty, of wood and perhaps not surprisingly it needed urgent repairs after the first winter. At this point major reconstruction took place, including the addition of a second tower. After incorporating various improvements Winstanley was happy with it; so chuffed, in fact, that he said he wanted to be there during a storm. He had to wait a few years, but in 1703 his wish was granted. He had to go anyway, to supervise yet more urgent repairs, but his timing proved fatal; the next day, this being November, there came the greatest storm ever to have been recorded in these lands. When it was over, little was left of the lighthouse and nothing was left of the occupants including

Winstanley. A rather sad ending to a five-year story.

Next up to the plate in 1706 was a silk merchant by the name of John Rudyerd, who also built a wooden structure, although it did prove more weather-worthy than Winstanley's effort, lasting as it did from 1709 until 1755. Fire was always a danger for these buildings, and that is what did for this version, despite efforts to put out the flames by its 94-year-old keeper, who managed to swallow some molten lead off the roof in the process as he gaped up at the conflagration above him. It should have killed him outright, but he and his mate were rescued and the old man lived for another 12 days. For five of those days the lighthouse blazed on until there was nothing left. So ended that attempt.

The seafarers who regularly used these waters were very concerned that once again they were to be deprived of the safety of having a working lighthouse, which they'd appreciated for the last 50-odd years. Now it was the turn of John Smeaton. His idea was to build a replacement – which would be number four – with a design on similar lines to an English oak tree, but made of stone. Local granite was plentiful and so too were sturdy Cornish labourers plucked from the tin mines. There was a problem, though. This was a time when much labour vanished at the hands of the press gangs, who kidnapped young fit men to serve on His Majesty's ships. Trinity House stepped in and saved the day with the issue of special badges stating that certain men were already seconded to work on the lighthouse construction and were on no account to be abducted by the press gangs. For those who saw working on the lighthouse as preferable to being sent to sea for an undefined period, I imagine some of those badges changed hands on the quiet, for a small consideration of course.

Having sorted out the manpower, there remained a few other

problems to sort out. The granite was a very strong rock, but this made it difficult to create dovetail joints in the stone. But they worked out how to do it, and the very same method is still used to this day. Next they had to find a way of making quick-setting cement, and a safe way of offloading hefty chunks of Cornwall's finest granite up onto the construction site from boats in a heaving swell. Patience and lots of brainwork solved these problems too, and the new Eddystone Lighthouse was completed with a lantern illuminated by 14 candles in the autumn of 1759. Quite apart from getting this project finished and working, Smeaton was also now the proud owner of a successful formula for quick-setting cement. This was the lighthouse that inspired the Bell Rock Lighthouse, among others. For well over a century it functioned well and would have continued to do so, had not cracks started to appear in the rock upon which it was built. The decision was taken to dismantle this long-serving edifice in the early 1880s, and rebuild it stone by stone at Plymouth Hoe as a monument to Smeaton. A stump of the original still remains on that cracked rock where once this mighty lighthouse stood.

Meanwhile, as soon as the cracks were spotted in the rock holding Smeaton's lighthouse in the 1870s, it became clear that a new lighthouse needed constructing on a different rocky base. On this occasion, for the fifth (and final) time, somebody had to come up with the goods as soon as possible. Trinity House charged their Engineer-in-Chief James Douglass with the job in 1877. Both design of lighthouses and construction methods had improved hugely over the 200 years since the first Eddystone lighthouse was built. Much of this was down to Stevenson, while the Frenchman Augustine Fresnel had invented a more sophisticated and efficient lighting system. Douglass stuck with the basic oak-tree idea, but used far larger stones, which were dovetailed in the now time-honoured way not only to each other on every side, but also now to each succeeding layer, which added to its strength. This version of the Eddystone Lighthouse, finished in 1882, is the one you see standing today. Just over 50 years ago, in 1956, its lantern was converted from oil to electricity. Some while later, in 1980, a helicopter pad was added, and two years after that the light station became fully automated and therefore unmanned from that day forward.

I can't resist staying in Cornwall, for a variety of reasons, including the folklore concerning the 'wreckers' of days gone by, who plundered stricken ships. Many ships fell foul of the lethal rocks that still lie in wait for the unwary, ready to ensnare them or impale them and then leave the sea to do the rest. Wreckers were always on the lookout for easy 'booty' – cargoes washed up on the shores that could be used right away, or taken away to be sold. If the natural elements didn't cause enough ships to be thrown onto the rocks in storms, then there was always the fallback of putting up false danger lights that actually drove ships onto the rocks rather than steering them safely by. If you have read Daphne du Maurier's book *Jamaica Inn*, you will be aware of some of the tales she told, although possibly one has to allow for a bit of artistic licence. I have a copy of this book that belonged to my grandmother, in which I found a hand-written postcard dated 1977 and part of a typewritten letter, both from Ms du Maurier.

The Cornish wreckers were a motley crew and apparently would not only plunder whatever came ashore, but would also remove the clothing from drowned sailors. (Apparently the wreckers of Cheshire and Liverpool were an even more ferocious lot, biting off the ears of shipwrecked corpses for the often valuable earrings that were worn in those days.) The wreckers' actions can be seen as a symptom of the plight that many people found themselves in. Times were hard and people had very little money. When an opportunity presented itself and the booty contained alcohol, then the normally restrained inhabitants of Marazion, Praa Sands, Porthleven, Prussia Cove and just about every coastal hamlet along the north or south Cornish coast would become bolder and find some release from their rather bleak and humdrum lives. They were tired of being under the heel of the customs men, who didn't care a bit about whatever hardships were caused by their relentless march filling the already huge coffers of the Crown, none of which ever seemed to find its way back to them. Plus ça change.

This reminds me of two much more recent occasions when there were huge arguments about salvage rights, both from a legal and moral perspective.

The first of these incidents was in January 2007, when the MSC *Napoli* container ship, en route from Antwerp to South Africa, came to grief in a storm off Sidmouth in Devon. The ship was holed, took on a huge amount of water very quickly and started to list heavily to starboard. The crew had to abandon ship – a very long and complicated affair as helicopters from RAF Culdrose had to winch each crew member off one by one in very stormy conditions. The drifting ship then started causing a hazard to other shipping, so the plan was to tow it to Portland Harbour for salvage. However, the boat's structure was severely compromised by the damage incurred, so it was decided instead to run it aground at Lyme Bay. There was some concern that about 150 of the nearly 2500 containers held hazardous goods, so the objective was to get these unloaded as soon as possible. There then followed a quite extraordinary sequence of events. Over 100 containers broke free and fell into the water, many of them floating onto the beaches at or around Branscombe. By now a veritable army of the curious, the adventurous and the plain greedy had collected on the cliffs and shoreline to see what could be had. The items of most value vanished first, of course, including an unknown quantity of brand new BMW motorbikes. The other items 'liberated' included barrels of wine, shoes, haircare products, beauty products and sundry car parts, such as gearboxes and steering wheels. Suddenly Branscombe was not only 'on the map' but was slipping back a couple of hundred years or so, as beachcombers – for want of a better term – descended onto the pebbles in their hundreds and helped themselves, without it crossing their minds that what they were doing was completely illegal. To them it was a simple case of 'finders keepers'. To others it was nothing short of looting. What they should have been doing was informing the Receiver of Wrecks of their soggy finds. Then a special form would have been provided that they would have completed and returned to the Receiver's Office within 28 days. Well, you can imagine how many – or should that be how few – would bother to go through all that red tape even if they knew of its existence. Something had to be done to close down this whole thing as it had rapidly got out of hand. The police closed the access roads and banned anyone from going onto the beach. There were also some ancient laws re-enacted that had not been used for a century or more forbidding cargo raids from taking place. It was rather a case of closing the stable door after the horse had bolted, stage left, pursued by bears.

The culmination of this strange episode occurred came five months later. Once all the cargo had been removed, it was soon discovered that the hope of refloating the ship was not an option after all, as the damage was worse than was earlier thought. The next option was to place explosive charges to split the ship in two: the first two attempts failed, but it worked at the third attempt. The agencies in charge of the clear-up operation were the Maritime Coastal Agency and the Ministry of Defence, and the cost of the whole long exercise escalated to a tidy £50 million.

Almost exactly a year after the *Napoli* foundered off Devon, the

Greek-registered *Ice Prince* came to grief off the Dorset coast. When she sank she shed about 2000 tons of timber into the brine. These 33-foot-long planks were in bundles and represented quite a serious hazard to others at sea until they began to break up into separate pieces in the rough water. When they were eventually washed up further east on Worthing beach, the inevitable happened: people zoomed in to the area and started loading as much as they could carry into whatever vehicles they could muster to take their plunder of planks away. After all the trouble from the previous year in Devon, the authorities were much quicker off the mark this time. The MCA warned that anyone caught taking away timber would be arrested and could be fined up to £2500. This time, too, the legalities were made more generally known, as the Merchant Shipping Act of 1995 clearly states that where washed-up cargo is concerned:

> "It is an offence to conceal or keep possession of such cargo, or to fail to report the cargo."

So, from these two stories, it is plain to see that the inbuilt rule of 'finders keepers' is alive and well – as I said, plus ça change.

Let's head to Wales now and visit another lighthouse. For around two centuries the Mumbles Lighthouse has been helping to keep shipping safe on the stretch of the Welsh coast leading to Swansea Harbour. Built on two small islands about 500 yards off the mainland, it is reachable on foot only when the tides allow; the remainder of the time access is only by boat. As with many lighthouses, it had a chequered early career as the first attempts to create a lasting structure failed. All was well by 1794 and the light was provided by two open coal fires (in braziers, which were both expensive and difficult to maintain). It was not long before it was fitted with a more efficient and safer oil-powered light, mounted in Argand lamps and amplified by reflectors. The British Transport Docks Board handed over responsibility of the lighthouse to Trinity House in 1975 and 20 years later Mumbles was converted to solar power.

The final stop in our historical tour of lighthouses is back in Cornwall, in my favourite part of that county, the Lizard, at the most southerly point of the British Isles. This lighthouse has the fairly unusual distinction of having two towers. The original tower was built in 1619 by a philanthropic Cornishman called Sir John Killigrew. Although he stumped up the cash for the construction, he could not afford the upkeep, so he imposed an annual rental of 20 nobles (almost £7) for a 30-year period, to be collected in voluntary contributions from ships that passed by. You can guess what happened – nobody paid. Contrary to advice from Trinity House, King James I imposed a levy of a halfpenny per ton on all passing marine traffic. Nobody paid this either, with the result that the light was extinguished and the lighthouse was pulled down, once again exposing shipping to the extreme dangers of this very tricky bit of coastline. Next in line for the onerous task of building a replacement was Thomas Fonnereau. He completed the building in 1751, and 20 years later Trinity House took over responsibility. The nearby signal station, built by Lloyd's of London, reported ships' arrivals, and so this lighthouse became the traditional landfall of all ships arriving in England, as it has remained for around 250 years. Structural alterations carried out in 1812 left the building very similar to that which you see today. The western tower ceased to be used just after 1903, leaving a single flashing light from the eastern tower. Automation was carried out in 1998. The lighthouse was closed for a while in 2004 for some renovations and then Trinity House took over responsibility for new visitor facilities and re-opened it in 2005. If you are down that way, the lighthouse is open every day during the summer, and several days each week during the remainder of the year.

I've talked about lighthouse designs but haven't said much about the lights inside them. The power of lighthouse beams is measured in terms of candlepower. This is probably the point to explain the meaning of one candlepower and one 'candela', which is the Latin for candle. Nobody seems to mention how large the candle was, but the assumption was that it was made of whale tallow burning at a specified rate in grains per hour. This all seems a bit haphazard to say the least. Maybe they thought so too, as this method of measurement was altered at least twice more, via some incredibly complicated formulae. Here, I hope, is the meaning in layman's language, although I will not be taking any questions afterwards: The current light inside the lighthouse at the Lizard produces a million candlepower. However, you might be surprised to hear that even in these days of advanced health and safety, the optic that produces the light floats in a bath of mercury. The light was powered by clockwork when it was manned, but now has a pair of electric motors. The bulb has to be replaced after 6000 hours and, like the motors, it is backed up in full auto mode.

Early in 2010 Trinity House made the shock announcement that it was actively considering turning off various lighthouses. Like shutting a theatre in London's West End, the lights would go out and they would 'fade to black'. Top of the reasons for closure was the greatly increased ownership of GPS systems, thanks to which fewer and fewer fishermen and other sea users need the aid of the lighthouses any longer. Top of the endangered list was the Beachy Head Lighthouse. Others with the sword of Damocles hanging over them were Orfordness in Suffolk, Blacknore Point in Somerset, Hartland Point in north Devon and Maryport in Cumbria. A spokesman for Trinity House made it plain that this was not being done for cost-cutting reasons but in recognition that the ceaseless

CANDLEPOWER

—

ONE CANDLEPOWER REPRESENTS THE
RADIATING CAPACITY OF A
LIGHT WITH THE INTENSITY OF ONE
'INTERNATIONAL CANDLE', OR
ABOUT 0.981 CANDELA AS NOW
DEFINED. OK SO FAR?

SINCE 1948 THE CANDELA HAS BEEN
THE OFFICIAL SI DERIVED UNIT
OF LIGHT INTENSITY, AND THE TERM
'CANDLEPOWER' NOW MEANS A
MEASUREMENT OF LIGHT INTENSITY
IN CANDELAS, JUST AS VOLTAGE MEANS
A MEASUREMENT OF ELECTRICAL
POTENTIAL IN VOLTS.

march of technology was rendering many of these sometimes unreliable lighthouses surplus to modern-day requirements. Sad though, when you think that on the cliffs of Beachy Head for instance, a light has beamed out as a warning to sailors since around 1670.

Time marches on, but if some lighthouses are no longer required for their intended purpose, hearteningly they may at least have an afterlife of sorts around the corner. The next time you are on holiday in Cornwall, or anywhere that has a lighthouse, and think to yourself: "Now that would be a mighty fine place to spend a couple of weeks or even the rest of my life..." It may surprise you to know that you can stay at some of these unusual locations, or even purchase them. At least one firm has teamed up with Trinity House to offer former lighthouse keepers' cottages around England, Wales and the Channel Islands. You can choose from Cornwall, Devon, Dorset, Kent, Wales, North Yorkshire and Alderney. Accommodation varies, but however many of you go, you are guaranteed some pretty fantastic views, living in part of this land's maritime fabric.

If you decide you are in the market to buy one of these amazing edifices, then let me give you an idea of what has been available in recent years. The first in my portfolio is the Corsewell Lighthouse in Kirkcolm. For over 185 years it has been warning shipping approaching the mouth of Loch Ryan of the rocks that lie ahead. It is still a working lighthouse, but the remainder of the buildings at its base – an award winning hotel – was on the market in 2008 for a cool £1.25 million. And what did you get for that? Six highly individually styled rooms, a dining room to seat 28 guests, 20 acres of grounds plus five recently renovated cottages that could be used on a self-catering basis. As for the views, well, to die for really: Arran, Ailsa Craig and the coast of Ireland. What's more it was all a going concern and – properly managed – would remain so for the lucky buyer.

In 2010 Port Lynas Lighthouse on Anglesey was put on the market for £1.5 million. This is a Grade II-listed building that the owners had spent 10 years restoring. It too is still in full automated working order, with its 1000W lamp casting a beam for more than 20 miles. At least one pod of dolphins are frequent visitors to the waters just below the tower, a sight you could never tire of. There is just one bum note, if you will excuse the pun: a very strident fog horn that sounds every 45 seconds when visibility is below two and a half miles. This could make for rather disjointed conversations, not to say disturbed sleep, but you might think on balance 'What the heck!'

The third and last on my books at the moment, the No Man's Land (Solent) Fort near Portsmouth was put on the market in 2008. 'For you, sir, that will be a round £4 million. It was built between 1861 and 1880 to house up to 80 soldiers to repulse any attack which might be forthcoming from the French. Not only was it a sort of Fort Bastion of the Solent, but also had 49 cannon onboard in addition to the all-important lighthouse. It was pretty much redundant by the time it was built, because the threat from the French had gone away. Used as an anti-aircraft battery during World War II, it was deactivated in 1956, and sold by the Ministry of Defence in 1986. It was used as a private residence during the 1990s, then converted into a five-star hotel with 21 rooms, along with a swimming pool, sauna, gym, restaurant and bars. It also had a central courtyard that was turned into an atrium. Its owner charged substantial rents of around £25,000 a day to large companies and corporations. Sadly he became ill, being diagnosed with Legionnaire's Disease, which he was thought to have contracted from contaminated water in the island well. The fort was quarantined, bringing the rentals to an abrupt halt and the absence of income suggested to the holding company that it was time to sell. Trouble was, not only was there Legionnaire's Disease in the well, but there were a few other flies in the ointment. The owner decided to dig his heels in, barricaded himself in the lighthouse and refused to leave. So, for sale, one lighthouse with three bedrooms, a sitting room with French windows opening onto a terrace offering a complete 360° view round the Solent – and a squatter; not a good selling point. By the way, you need to own or be able to afford to hire a helicopter to get there, as the boat winch is broken – damn it.

I will remove my estate agent's hat now – that last one was a bit off the wall, but true nonetheless. I must admit, however, that I did work in a London estate agents' office in my first job, many moons ago. The most exciting thing that happened to me while in that job revolved around the Christine Keeler affair, which led to the fall of the MacMillan Government, a suicide, gunshots in Wimpole Mews late one night, and goodness knows what else. But that is certainly another story altogether. The BBC seemed quite tame in comparison, well, to begin with anyway.

I did say at the start of this chapter that there were some spooky goings-on to recount. All these stories emanate from Scotland, in fact. First stop is Dundee, and although I know there is not much evidence of lighthouses on the way to the Antarctic, I had to include this one. Berthed here is the Royal Research Ship (RRS) *Discovery*, which was launched in 1901 and used by the Antarctic explorers Scott and Shackleton. After all this time, it seems that one former crew member is reluctant to leave ship and that there is a ghost on board. Footsteps have been heard and a figure spotted. It could be Shackleton, or perhaps Charles Bonner, a member of the crew who plummeted to his death from the dizzy heights of the crow's nest. We will probably never know.

The next spooky tale is from the Eilean Mor Lighthouse on the Outer Hebrides. This is one of the most isolated lighthouses anywhere, and the scene of one of the most intriguing mysteries in Scottish history. You have heard the tale of the *Mary Celeste*, a deserted ship on the high seas? Well, bear that in mind. On Boxing Day in 1900, a lighthouse vessel visited the Eilean Mor Lighthouse because the light had not been seen flashing for several days and there was concern for the three keepers. The relief keeper went ashore to the lighthouse to find out what was wrong. The doors were closed, the clock had stopped, there were no fires burning and the last entry in the log was about 10 days before. Most importantly and strangely, there was no sign of the three keepers, and the lighthouse rowing boat was missing from its mooring. An entry in the logbook told of a really fierce storm, when one of the keepers was so scared that he was in tears and on his knees praying for his life. However there was also a record that the storm passed and that the sea was once again calm. One possible explanation of the mysterious disappearances is that a huge wave caught all three keepers while they were struggling with a faulty crane gantry, and washed them into the sea. If this was not the case then why did they 'abandon ship', as it were, and what became of them? No bodies were ever found.

Finally there is the Ardnamurchan Lighthouse. Does this sound a bit familiar to you? Built by Alan Stevenson of lighthouse family fame, in an unusual Egyptian style, it was completed in 1849 and I gather was the inspiration for *Pharos*, a ghost story by Alice Thompson. The local story is that in the 19th century all three keepers from this lighthouse vanished. Like those at Eilean Mor, they were never seen again.

To end on a lighter note, some years ago a lighthouse was attacked by vandals with many gallons of pink and yellow paint. The lighthouse in question was the Port Appin on the west coast of Scotland. It was a case of Mr Blobby fights back. Yes, it was pink with yellow spots, not the colour scheme mandated by the Northern Lighthouse Board. An adjoining storage building was also painted in matching new livery. The authorities failed to see the funny side of the event and right away flew a supply of white paint to the lighthouse by helicopter, to have it returned to its normal white appearance. All shipping in the area was warned that the Port Appin lighthouse was wearing new garb, but only temporarily (all lighthouses are marked or painted differently and can be looked up to check that the one you are looking at really is the one you think it is). I would think that the repainting was probably done in record time and Mr Blobby was consigned to oblivion.

TWELVE

—

CODES, CONVENTIONS AND TRADITIONS

Now let's look a little deeper into the dark art of Morse Code, and wireless telegraphy generally, and learn just why it became so useful (even though when I was younger I failed to understand more than dot dot dot – dash dash dash – dot dot dot, or SOS, the internationally recognised distress signal code).

The word *wireless* was the forerunner of the word *radio*, and the term *wireless telegraphy* was introduced to described electrical signalling without the use of wires, to avoid confusion with the electric telegraph, which did require wires to connect the sender and receiver. It is all a far cry from sending smoke signals, lighting beacons or using talking drums, heliographs and flag semaphore. In the 18th and early 19th centuries there were many attempts both in England and America to create a new system, using whatever technology was around at the time. Most of these systems had to be abandoned for one reason or another – more often than not to do with cost. Then in 1836 three Americans, the artist Samuel B. Morse, the physicist Joseph Henry, and the machinist and inventor Alfred Vail, got together and set about developing what was to become the all-important electric telegraph system. It sent a pulsing electrical current through wires, which activated an audible clicking mechanism at the receiving end. A year later, two Englishmen contrived another system that used needles to point at the relevant letters of the alphabet rather than using audio clicks. However, this had a far more limited application, and didn't prove at all successful. (Having said that, the earliest Morse Code was printed on paper tape so that it could be *read*, but it soon became clear that this layer of intelligibility could be done away with when the operators became more and more proficient at learning Morse as a language to be heard rather than read from the printed (or in this case *indented*) page.) Aviators benefited from using Morse Code from the 1920s, although as late as 1927, when Charles Lindbergh made his historic flight from New York to Paris, radio telegraph was not universal in planes, so he was on his own once he had taken off. In the 1930s, the first flight from California to Australia was made much safer as one of the crew acted as radio operator, keeping in touch with the ground via radio telegraph. From around this time, aeroplane pilots, military and civilian, had to be proficient in Morse Code, so they could use the communication systems, and also for navigation. Navigational beacons now used two or three-letter identifiers so that, in conjunction with aeronautical charts, pilots could find their way to the next mapped location.

Alongside radio telegraphy, radio telephony (voice radio) became more widely used in the 1920s as the quality rapidly improved. However, Morse really came into its own during World War II as it was soon found that voice radio systems were not only unusable over anything but quite short distances but were also open to being overheard by the enemy. Morse Code messages, encrypted for security, were used extensively by the British between warships and Royal Naval bases, as well as by the German Navy, the Imperial Japanese Navy, the Royal Canadian Navy, the Royal Australian Navy, the US Navy and the US Coastguard.

Morse Code continued in use as a standard international maritime means of communication until as recently as 1999. No longer used on a day-to-day basis on the high seas, there are still some occasions when Morse can play its part if all other forms of communication have broken down, though this is increasingly unlikely of course.

Communications and positioning systems developed rapidly in the latter years of the 20th century. In 1999 Morse was replaced internationally by the Global Maritime Distress Safety System (GMDSS). Based on both existing and new technologies, its primary functions are to determine the location of ships, aircraft or persons in distress (and thus enable search and rescue co-ordination to proceed), to transmit maritime safety broadcasts, and for bridge-to-bridge communications. It enables both ship-to-ship and ship-to-shore contact. GMDSS is used by the military and by commercial shipping, both freight and passenger. Smaller craft, used for recreational purposes, do not have to comply with GMDSS, and are more likely to use Digital Selective Calling (DSC) on their VHF radios.

Another handy (not to say potentially lifesaving) bit of kit is the satellite-based Emergency Position Indicating Radio Beacon (EPIRB), which is required equipment on commercial fishing vessels and all passenger liners. If there is a problem anywhere in the world, rescue co-ordinates are sent via satellite, so the nearest rescue services would know within seconds exactly where that vessel is, and can start organising appropriate action. The latest GPS receivers can pinpoint a vessel to within 20 metres, somewhat better than the three nautical miles of just a few years ago.

There is also Navtex, another internationally-used automated system for shipping, designed for the instant dissemination of navigational warnings, weather forecasts and warnings, plus search and rescue information to all interested parties.

So nowadays we are most likely to hear Morse Code on TV – as Barrington Pheloung cleverly incorporated the SOS rhythm in his music for the popular Inspector Morse series. It's still available on various TV channels if you have the posh equipment to receive them.

Posh. What a word – and what a misunderstood and misused word in maritime circles. I had always understood it to be an acronym for *Port Out, Starboard Home*, relating to the preferred cabin location on British ships travelling to and from India in the late 19th century. The idea was to always be on the north-facing, shaded side of the ship, away from the blazing sun – in other words to be on the left (port) side on the way to India and on the right (starboard) side on the way home. This explanation for the derivation of 'posh' is unproven, however, and pooh-poohed by various authorities. But even if this isn't the real explanation, the concept of 'Port Out, Starboard Home' was all about having choice, and access to accommodation that was costly, elegant, exclusive, expensive, first or upper class, grand, luxurious, opulent, palatial, rich, ritzy, select, splendid, sumptuous and swanky. These are all synonyms for the present-day meaning of *posh*, and sum up what sea travel could be for those that could afford it in olden days. However (and there is always a however), the more likely derivation of *posh* is from the now obsolete word for a dandy, which also carries a long list of unflattering etymological synonyms: a ninny, silly fellow, one who plays the fool, dresses in finery to draw undue attention, a fop, a coxcomb. Interestingly, two other words that come out of this have a distinctly waterborne feel to them: *yawl* and *ketch*. Both are names for two-masted sailing vessels that are rigged fore and aft, with a large main mast, and a small mizzenmast aft of the rudder post.

Hope *yawl* happy with that. Sounds to me as though they are somewhat overdressed for whatever occasion they were to be involved in – or am I mizzen the point? Anyway we like the cut of their jib.

But for how long have we been calling the sides of a ship *port* and *starboard*, and why? Starboard originated with the Vikings, who have a lot to answer for one way and another. They called the side of a ship a *board*, and the steering oar or *styri* was at the back on the right-hand side of the ship. In Old English the left side was called *baecbord* (i.e. back board – the side behind the steerer); in Middle English this changed to *laddeborde* (thought to mean load board – the side a ship that was usually used for loading), which in turn changed to *larboard*. This sounded too much like starboard, so usage was changed gradually from the 17th century to *port side* (still referring to the loading of the ship, and either meaning the harbour side of the ship or derived from the Latin word porta for *gate* or *entrance*). Over the years this was then further shortened to just *port*.

The Italian for port and starboard sounds really splendid, but then it is such a lovely language. Starboard is questa borda, meaning *this side*, and port is quella borda, meaning (I'm sure you can see it coming) 'that side'. Hmm, well… as long as they understand.

Let's take a look now at another maritime convention – the use of the colours red and green in navigation. Do you know which means left and which means right? If you're unsure, just remember that port is left and red (think of port wine), so therefore green is right. But how did this convention come about? For a long, long time ships have deemed it prudent to carry some sort of light to show at night. For much of that time it tended to be a white light, and only one light at that – which in sum total was probably not that helpful to any other craft that were around at the time. Eventually, no doubt after several collisions, national maritime authorities decided to impose some regulation, but at first these varied in different countries. In 1824 the Dutch authorities required ships to show two white lights after dark. In 1840 Trinity House came up with the rather good idea that if two steam vessels found themselves heading towards one another at night, they should take the following avoiding action: each alter course to starboard, keeping the oncoming ship to the port side. This was codified in the Steam Navigation Act 1846. In 1848 the Admiralty ordered all steamships to be fitted with red and green lights, selected as eye-catching and completely different to each other – unless you are colour-blind, of course. The USA adopted the same rules the following year, and these regulations were extended to sailing vessels in 1858. Clearly a co-ordinated approach was needed, however, so in 1864 Britain and France agreed a more comprehensive set of navigation rules, called the Articles, and sent them to other major maritime nations; more than 30 countries adopted these regulations. New rules were implemented in 1884, and then the first International Maritime Conference was held in 1889 in Washington, D.C., which agreed a fresh set of regulations. Minor changes were made to these by the Brussels International Maritime Conference in 1910, and by the series of Safety of Life at Sea conferences, the first of which was convened in response to the 1912 sinking of the *Titanic*. From 1953 the rules were also applied to aircraft.

Nowadays, navigation rules are governed by the International Regulations for Preventing Collisions at Sea, adopted at a convention of the International Maritime Organization in 1972. Under this system all marine vessels (and aircraft too) are lit with what are called *right of way lights* in the following way. A side-and-front-facing red light is mounted on the left side, a green is on the right, and a white light is on the stern (though the white stern light doesn't appear on aircraft). The safety code states that if two ships are heading for each other after dark and the pilot sees the green light, he knows he is on the other craft's starboard side and has the right of way. If he sees the red port light, the other craft has the right of way as it is to his port side, and his vessel must alter course to avoid a collision. If the pilot sees only a white light ahead of him, then there's a sigh of relief all round as he knows that both he and the other ship are going in the same direction. If the pilot sees both the red and green lights at zero degrees then it may well be time to abandon ship as both vessels are clearly on a collision course with little or no time to alter their path!

There's one more interesting aspect of the use of green and red that I'm going to mention (though it's not related to shipping or the Shipping Forecast at all!) and that's ink. Various Commanders-in-Chief of the Armed Forces have used these colours when writing to each other or to their subordinates. Indeed, I gather that some still do. Sir John Scarlett, the previous head of MI6 – or SIS as it is officially called – always signed himself 'C' in green ink on official SIS documents. There is some precedent for this: the first head of the secret service, Captain Sir George Mansfield Smith-Cumming RN, always signed himself either *CM* or simply *C* in green ink. All subsequent Chiefs of that service have become known as *C* and continued to use green ink. So, for over a hundred years now (the service was set up in 1909), the signature of the chief incumbent and the colour of the ink have remained the same – a sure-fire example of a tradition if ever there was one.

A former First Lord of the Admiralty always wrote his missives in red ink, so that the recipients would know immediately who it was from. In turn the First Sea Lord would respond in green ink, which was rather a nice touch. In 1964 First Lords of the Admiralty ceased to be, when the Navy came under the wing of the Ministry of Defence, thereby making the Queen the Lord High Admiral. (History doesn't relate what colour of ink Her Majesty uses, but I suspect it is neither of these.)

It's strange to think of these illustrious heads of our services being so particular about the colour of their missives, and even stranger that so many have been fond of green when in other walks of life writing in green ink has been apt to attract the wrong sort of attention. Today, we have what are known as *the green ink brigade* who use green when writing to complain to authority or to vent their spleen at some perceived shortcoming of goods or services. I had my share of this when I was broadcasting on Radio 4. Before opening an envelope addressed in this colour, you had ample warning of what was to come – and were seldom wrong. Such letters usually lacked logic and basic facts by the truckload, and one just hoped that the sender felt better after writing their bilious screed.

We have had a look at some codes and conventions coupled with etiquette; how about a general look at naval terms used in our everyday speech, which have nautical origins. I can't resist selecting a few for your perusal. I will attempt to keep them ship shape and Bristol fashion of course.

I found a few matters of interest including the meaning of the word to measure the speed of vessels across or through the water. I am of course talking about the Knot. It is rather complicated to explain, so I will opt for the short cut by saying that it was to do with how many knots were tied on a line that passed through the seaman's hand over a certain time. It was then possible to calculate the speed of the boat and it was expressed in Knots or knots per hour. I hope that will suffice. I think to have told the full explanation would most certainly have tied me in knots and probably left you none the wiser. We have heard about the cat o' nine tails, but what about the feline that often became the ship's cat? I wonder if the two are connected insofar as a cat is said to have nine lives. If a cat was taken on board, it was almost regarded as crew, as it was expected to earn its keep by keeping down the most obvious vermin, that being rats and mice which were often *imported* along with the provisions in port as they were loaded for the voyage. I don't know if they still exist, but there was a type of cat which had an extra digit on each foot. They were labelled as Polydactyl cats and this extra grip was very useful for killing prey and had good sea legs. Cats have always been thought of as rather like a *good luck* charm on a ship. They were always liked by the crews and were never short of attention, so a two way profit for man and beast. It is thought that having cats on ships goes back as far as the Phoenicians about nine centuries ago, who brought the first domesticated cats into Europe.

Cats have served in the navy in more recent times. In World War II there was a very much loved and successful ratter on HMS *Amethyst*, which was shelled by the communists in the Yangtse River in 1949. The cat's name was Simon and he had a rank – that of Able Seaman. He was badly injured in the attack and the story got around, that although poor Simon survived his injuries against all expectation, he died whilst in quarantine awaiting repatriation to the UK. He was posthumously awarded the Dickin Medal which is the animal version of the Victoria Cross.

Ginger and *Fishcakes* were two serving cats on HMS *Hood* between 1933-1935. I have not been able to discover if they perished amongst those on board in 1941. I daresay' health and safety' brought an end to having cats on naval vessels. Whatever the cause or reason, the Royal Navy banned them back in 1975.

AS THE CROW FLIES

—

ONCE UPON A TIME IT WAS USUAL
TO CARRY CROWS ABOARD
SHIPS SO THAT WHEN OUT OF SIGHT
OF DRY LAND A CROW WOULD
BE RELEASED BECAUSE IT ALWAYS TOOK
THE MOST DIRECT LINE TO THE
NEAREST SHORE. WAS THEIR SUPERIOR
EYESIGHT THE REASON FOR THEIR
SKILL, ONCE UP IN THE AIR WITH THE
HORIZON IN VIEW, OR DO THEY
JUST HAVE AN EXTRA SENSE THAT
WE DO NOT POSSESS?

SHIPS WOULD FOLLOW THE CROW,
WITH A MAN AS LOOK OUT, UP
IN THE HIGHEST PART OF THE VESSEL
WHICH BECAME KNOWN AS THE
'CROW'S NEST'.

AND NOW THE SHIPPING FORECAST

AT LOGGERHEADS

—

A LOGGERHEAD COMPRISED AN
IRON BALL ON THE END OF A
LONG HANDLE WHICH WAS USED
TO HEAT PITCH FOR REPAIRING
THE SEALING BETWEEN THE
DECK PLANKS

ON OCCASION, WHEN AN
ARGUMENT BROKE OUT
THESE ITEMS WERE SOMETIMES
USED AS WEAPONS.

BETWEEN THE
DEVIL AND
THE DEEP BLUE SEA

—

THE LONGEST SEAM OF THE SHIP
THAT RAN FROM STEM TO STERN
ALONG THE BEAM WHICH SUPPORTED
THE GUN DECK WAS CALLED
'THE DEVIL'

TO SEAL THIS SEAM WHILST AT SEA,
SOME POOR UNFORTUNATE
WOULD BE SUSPENDED OVER THE
SIDE OF THE SHIP TO MAKE
THE REPAIR – SO HE REALLY WAS
BETWEEN THE 'DEVIL' AND
THE DEEP BLUE SEA.

AND NOW THE SHIPPING FORECAST

CHEWING

THE FAT

—

TO PRESERVE THE MEAT STOCKS
ON BOARD SHIP, IT ALL HAD TO BE
SALTED. THE DOWNSIDE WAS THAT IT
MADE THE MEAT VERY TOUGH TO
CHEW, SO PROLONGED MASTICATION
WAS REQUIRED TO MAKE IT EDIBLE.

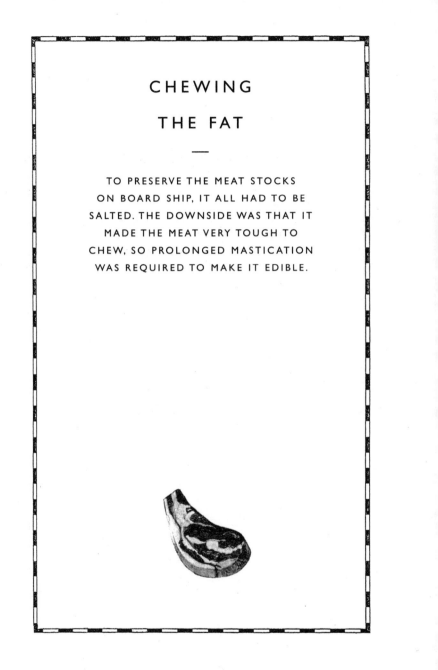

DOWN

THE

HATCH

—

CAME FROM THE FACT THAT
ALL CARGOES HAD TO BE LOADED
DOWN INTO THE HOLD THROUGH
HATCHES ON DECK, GIVING THE
IMPRESSION THAT THEY WERE BEING
CONSUMED BY THE SHIP.

DUTCH

COURAGE

—

WHICH STEMS FROM THE ANGLO-
DUTCH WARS IN THE SEVENTEENTH
CENTURY. A DESCRIPTIVE PHRASE
THAT INCLUDED THE WORD 'DUTCH'
OR 'GO DUTCH', 'DUTCH UNCLE',
AND 'DOUBLE DUTCH', WAS USED
AS AN INSULT.

THE WORD WENT ABOUT BY WAY
OF ENGLISH PROPAGANDA THAT
DUTCH SAILORS AND TROOPS WERE
SO COWARDLY THAT THEY COULD
ONLY FIGHT WHEN DRUNK
ON SCHNAPPS.

GROGGY

—

ADMIRAL EDWARD VERNON WAS
RATHER CONCERNED AT THE
CONSTANT DRUNKENNESS OF HIS
CREWS AND SO DECREED IN 1740
THAT THE DAILY RUM RATION
BE DILUTED. THIS SOON BECAME THE
NORM THROUGHOUT THE NAVY.

MANY OF THE SEAMEN WERE LESS THAN
HAPPY ABOUT THIS INFRINGEMENT
OF WHAT THEY SAW AS THEIR 'RIGHTS'
AND FROM THEN ON REFERRED TO
VERNON AS 'OLD GROG' AFTER HIS
COATS WHICH WERE MADE OF
GROGRAM – A COURSE MIXTURE OF
WOOL AND MOHAIR STIFFENED WITH
GUM. THE WEAKER ALLOWANCE OF RUM
BECAME KNOWN AS 'GROG' AND
SOMEBODY WHO HAD SOMEHOW
MANAGED TO GET MORE THAN THEIR
FAIR SHARE WAS TERMED AS 'GROGGY'.

AND NOW THE SHIPPING FORECAST

NO

GREAT

SHAKES

—

RELATED TO EMPTY CASKS OF SAID
GROG WHICH WERE TAKEN TO
PIECES OR 'SHAKEN' SO THAT THEY
COULD BE STORED MORE EASILY,
TAKING UP LESS VALUABLE AND ALWAYS
LIMITED SPACE. THE COMPONENT
PARTS OF A BARREL – THE STAVES AND
HOOPS HAD NO FURTHER USE OR
VALUE AND WERE KNOWN AS 'SHAKES'.

THREE SHEETS TO THE WIND

—

A SHEET WAS A ROPE USED TO CONTROL A SAIL. THERE WERE TIMES WHEN, PARTICULARLY IN HEAVY WEATHER, A SHEET COULD BECOME DAMAGED AND THE MORE THAT WERE DAMAGED, ALLOWING THE SAIL TO BILLOW, THE MORE DIFFICULT IT BECAME TO REGAIN CONTROL OF THE SHIP.

SO IT CAME ABOUT THAT A SAILOR IN VARIOUS STAGES OF INEBRIATION WAS DESCRIBED AS BEING ONE OR TWO SHEETS TO THE WIND. IF HE WAS THREE SHEETS TO THE WIND, HE WAS PRETTY SOZZLED.

EAT

MY HAT

—

STEMMED FROM THE SAILORS KEEPING
THEIR CHEWING TOBACCO IN
THEIR HATS. THESE MUST HAVE BECOME
SOMEWHAT INSANITARY AS THE
LININGS BECAME SOAKED IN SWEAT
AND SPITTLE MIXED WITH THE
JUICE FROM THE CHEWED TOBACCO.

IF THE WORST HAPPENED, AND THEY
RAN OUT OF TOBACCO, THE
SAILORS WOULD REMOVE THE LININGS
OF THEIR HATS AND CHEW THEM.

LET THE
CAT OUT
OF THE BAG

—

WAS ABOUT THE FEARED PUNISHMENT
ON BOARD OF THE 'CAT O' NINE
TAILS', WHICH BEFORE AND AFTER USE
WAS KEPT IN A CLOTH BAG. WHEN
FLOGGINGS DID OCCUR THEY TOOK
PLACE ON DECK, AS THERE WAS NOT
ENOUGH SPACE BELOW DECKS TO METE
OUT THIS PUNISHMENT.

IN OTHER WORDS THERE WAS NOT
ENOUGH ROOM TO 'SWING A CAT'.

PRESS

INTO SERVICE

—

CAME FROM THE ACT OF SEIZING
PRIVATE GOODS AND PROPERTY
FOR PUBLIC SERVICE AND IT ALSO
RELATED TO FORCING MEN
AGAINST THEIR WILL TO WORK FOR
THE NAVY FOR AN INDEFINITE
AMOUNT OF TIME. PRESS GANGS
TRICKED OR SIMPLY KIDNAPPED
MEN, QUITE OFTEN ON THEIR WAY
OUT OF A TAVERN LATE AT NIGHT,
INTO SERVING 'KING AND COUNTRY'.

SHIP SHAPE

&

BRISTOL FASHION

—

BRISTOL HAD A VERY GOOD NAME
FOR ITS HIGH STANDARDS OF SHIPPING
AND EQUIPMENT.

THE DOCKS WERE BUILT IN THE MID
NINETEENTH CENTURY, BUT
BEFORE THEN THERE WAS ROUGHLY
A TEN METER VARIANCE BETWEEN
HIGH AND LOW TIDES, SO SHIPS
STRANDED DURING LOW TIDE ON THE
EXPOSED SEABED HAD TO BE VERY
STURDILY BUILT TO WITHSTAND THE
PRESSURES CAUSED BY THEIR
UNSUPPORTED WEIGHT. THEIR CARGOES
HAD TO BE PARTICULARLY
SECURELY FASTENED.

TURN A BLIND EYE

—

WAS DOWN TO LORD NELSON AT THE
BATTLE OF COPENHAGEN IN 1801,
HIS HARDEST FOUGHT VICTORY, WHEN
HE WAS TOLD HE WAS BEING
SIGNALLED BY THE ADMIRAL OF THE
FLEET. HE PUT HIS TELESCOPE UP
TO HIS BLIND EYE AND DENIED SEEING
ANY SUCH ORDER. HIS REASON WAS
THAT IF HE HAD OBEYED THE ORDER,
HE WOULD HAVE PUT MANY OF HIS
SHIPS IN DANGER IN NEARBY
SHALLOW WATERS.

MANY BELIEVE THAT WHEN HE PUT
THE TELESCOPE TO HIS BLIND
EYE HE SAID 'I SEE NO SHIPS' BUT THIS
IS NOT TRUE. PITY, BUT THERE WE
ARE. AT LEAST IT SHOWS HE HAD A
SENSE OF HUMOUR, AND WAS
CERTAINLY MINDFUL OF THE SAFETY
OF HIS MEN AND SHIPS.

SPLICING

THE

MAINBRACE

—

WAS AN ARDUOUS AND BIG JOB TO
HAVE TO DO, USUALLY IN A BIT
OF A HURRY, AS THIS WAS THE LARGEST
AND HEAVIEST BIT OF RIGGING ON
BOARD AND KEY TO THE WHOLE OF A
SAILING SHIP'S BALANCE.

SO WHEN IT WAS DAMAGED, AND IT
WAS OFTEN A TARGET OF ENEMY
CANNONS IN BATTLES, IT NEEDED
INSTANT REPAIR. FAILURE TO DO SO
WOULD RESULT IN THE SHIP BEING
BECALMED AND AN EASY TARGET FOR
THE ENEMY TO FINISH OFF. A
SUCCESSFUL OPERATION EARNED THE
CREW INVOLVED IN ITS REPAIR AN
EXTRA TOT OF RUM.

IT HAS SINCE BEEN COINED AS A
PHRASE TO TROT OUT ON A MAJOR
OCCASION OR CELEBRATION WHEN A
BOTTLE OR TWO NEEDS OPENING.

HOWEVER IN THE NAVY, ONLY THE
QUEEN COULD GIVE PERMISSION
FOR THE MAIN BRACE TO BE SPLICED.
FAILING HER, IT COULD BE ANOTHER
MEMBER OF THE ROYAL FAMILY OR THE
ADMIRALTY BOARD.

THINGS HAVE BEEN RELAXED NOW
AND AS RUM HAS NOT BEEN ISSUED
ON A DAILY BASIS SINCE 1990, THERE
ARE OTHER TIMES WHEN AN ORDER
IS GIVEN WHICH MIGHT IN THE
PAST NOT HAVE BEEN DEEMED TO
WARRANT THIS COMMAND.

I am not sure if those naval felines were fed anything other than what they caught for themselves. But one item which comes to mind is the famous *Ship's Biscuits*. It's less of a problem today of course with refrigeration plants on ships to preserve foodstuffs on long voyages. In earlier times, fresh food had to be kept to a minimum or else salted to preserve it. A certain amount of what one had to call *live* food was taken aboard including sheep and poultry, but as space was at something of a premium, there were limits and as for hygiene etc, well, best not to think about that too deeply. This meant that the ship's compliment had to include a butcher and a cook, two more people on an already crowded ship. The partial answer to a more varied and yet balanced diet was to come up with something that was dry and would keep *fresh*. There is certainly nothing new in needing some non-perishable food stuffs that were easy to transport without taking up too much room but which were, at least to some extent, a means of providing some nourishing fodder for armies and navies on the move. Egyptian sailors carried some maize bread, and the Romans had a form of biscuit. Richard the Lionheart on the third Crusade between 1189 – 1192 carried a *Biskit* which was made of barley, rye and bean flour. A bit later in 1588 at the time of the Armada, there was a daily allowance of a pound of biscuits and the all important gallon of beer. I must say a gallon of beer does sound rather a lot, but there we are. *Hardtack* was what the British sailors called them, and probably derived from their slang word for food being *Tack*. They were also known – with good reason – as *dog biscuits, tooth dullers, sheet iron* and *molar breakers*. I'm sure they had their advantages, but I am equally sure they must have kept the ship's surgeon busy when he wasn't hacking off damaged limbs etc. Anyway biscuits of many and varied recipes, including those which contained seed and dried fruit, were to remain as a very important part of a sailor's day to day diet right up until the advent of canned foods in the 1840s. Certainly up to about ten years ago, the MOD purchased biscuits for a part of operational ration packs. I suspect though that this was for the Army rather than the Navy. Whatever they tasted like, probably of precious little most of the time, they were duly chewed and swallowed, giving at least a modicum of nourishment.

Well, it's time to *swallow the anchor*, which in naval terms means it's time to leave the sea and have no further use for that rather important item that you have relied on. We are weighing anchor and moving on to Greenwich and a quick look at time as we know it.

THIRTEEN

—

TIME AND GREENWICH MEAN TIME

We are all used to what we know as local time, no matter where in the world we live. Local time depends on the rising and setting of the sun and the longitude and latitude of where we are. Even within the UK, small though it is, geographical midday in London is some 20 minutes ahead of geographical midday in Land's End, for instance. The further east you travel, the further advanced the local time becomes. As society became more mobile with the advent of rail travel, it became more confusing to know the local time during your journey and at your destination. It was soon realised that it would make people's lives a lot less complicated if a whole country, or large parts of it, used a standard time. An international solution was needed. By the 1880s most mariners and map-makers were using the meridian (line of longitude, where the sun passes overhead at midday) through Greenwich in the UK as the Prime Meridian – where east meets west, defining 0° longitude. So, in 1884, when representatives from 25 nations got together in Washington, D.C., for the International Meridian Conference, they agreed upon taking the Greenwich meridian as the Prime Meridian and specifed that Greenwich Mean Time should be used as the global time standard. International time zones relative to GMT were subsequently adopted, and this is how things have remained (with the odd time-zone tweak here or there).

The questions that leap out are why 'Greenwich' and why 'Mean Time?' Let's start with the second part. We all know it takes 24 hours for the Earth to perform one full rotation on its axis – but that's not quite true as the tilt of the Earth's axis and unevenness in the speed of the Earth's orbit round the sun causes the length of each day to vary by as much as 30 seconds. Next fact – the Earth takes 365 days to complete each journey round the sun. Well I'm sure you're ahead of me now: it is more like 365 and a quarter days, which is why every four years we have a leap year to add a day. However, the real difference is not quite a quarter of a day each year – so further adjustment is needed, namely that centuries (e.g. 1700, 1800, 1900) are not leap years.

All of these non-uniformities are averaged out to give a *mean* time for us to use – which results in 1200 Greenwich Mean Time differing by as much as 16 minutes from actual midday at Greenwich, the time when the sun is directly overhead the Prime Meridian.

You may have come across the term Universal Time (UT). Be not afraid, this is in essence just another way of saying GMT, brought in to clear up an ambiguity that had become associated with GMT. This was that before 1925, sailors and astronomers counted time from midday so 0000 GMT for them was 1200 GMT for the rest of us. This created a bit of confusion, as you can imagine, so astronomers agreed in 1925 that the civil GMT and the astronomical GMT should be synchronised, with each day starting at midnight. However, confusion continued, so in 1928 the new name of Universal Time was introduced as the preferred term.

That was fine for a while and then in the 1950s along came atomic clocks, which could measure time to an accuracy of within one second in a million years. The first caesium-based atomic clock was built in 1955 by Louis Essen at the National Physical Laboratory in the UK. As the measurement of GMT was based on astronomical observations of the Earth's position in relation to other celestial bodies, it would never keep time as accurately as these atomic clocks measuring International Atomic Time.

The problem here is that *terrestrial time* and *atomic time* are not the same thing at all. *Terrestrial time* is locked in with the rotation of the earth, which is not anything like as constant as you may think. It has blips and wobbles and varies more than the unerringly-accurate 'atomic time' will allow for. After much head-scratching and many sleepless nights, the boffins came up with Co-ordinated Universal Time (UTC), which was adopted in 1972 as the world's time standard, replacing GMT for official use. UTC is based on International Atomic Time, but has leap seconds added at irregular intervals, to compensate for the slowing down of the Earth's rotation and keep it within a second of GMT. Currently (in January 2011) UTC is International Atomic Time minus 34 seconds. A leap second can only be added (or subtracted – but this has never yet been necessary) at midnight on the last day of June or December; the decision on whether a leap second is needed is made by the International Earth Rotation Service (IERS).

Computers and the scientific fraternity specify time in UTC as they need this level of accuracy, but in most walks of life the terms UTC and GMT can be used interchangeably, and GMT is still the legal civil term in the UK. You may be surprised to hear that the aviation industry and some radio broadcasters (including the BBC World Service) also use UTC, but the main reason for this is that it is never adjusted for daylight saving time.

BST (British Summer Time) was already in use before the BBC came into being. Originally it was called Summer Time or Daylight Saving Time. It began in 1916 as a wartime measure to save energy, and was made official when the Summer Time Acts were passed by Parliament in 1922 and 1925, lengthening evening daylight from spring to autumn by moving the clock one hour ahead of GMT. During World War II double summertime was introduced as a further energy-saving measure: the clocks were two hours ahead of GMT in summer, and one hour ahead of GMT during the winter months. There was a certain amount of tinkering in the post-war years, altering the dates when summertime began and ended continued right up to 1998. Since then, British Summer Time has always begun on the last Sunday in March and ended on the last Sunday in October. The time of the change was agreed at 0100 in the morning. So here we are nearly a century on, still playing with our clocks twice a year and cursing the advent of the dark winter evenings. While many of us wish that we could have summertime all year round, Scotland has always fought against this idea. In the depths of winter the days are even shorter in northern climes, so schoolchildren and workers – particularly in the north west – would have to travel in darkness until about 1000. Longer evenings, yes, but a poor start to the day.

But you're still waiting to get the answer to: why 'Greenwich?' Why on earth was this tiny place on the River Thames chosen to have this special distinction? The reasons for this included the existence of the Royal Observatory at Greenwich, which by 1884 had become renowned as a centre of excellence for accurate timekeeping and astronomical research. Since 1833 the 'Time Ball' on the original observatory building, Flamsteed House, had been providing a time signal that was relied upon by ships on the Thames and by everyone throughout the capital. GMT had been the accepted time standard for both the UK and the

USA since 1880 (by the late 1800s all shipping relied on it). Further afield, nearly three-quarters of global commerce used sea charts that had Greenwich marked as the Prime Meridian. The combination of all these facts made Greenwich the obvious choice, even though places such as San Domingo, France and Brazil were left unconvinced – at least for a few more years.

We can't leave the subject of Greenwich and the time without mentioning the Greenwich Time Signal (GTS) – or the Pips as many people call them. Anyone listening to BBC Radio over the years can't fail to have heard this time signal many times over. So how did that all begin and why?

The BBC was formed of a consortium of companies in 1922, including Marconi, Western Electric and General Electric. When the BBC was all but a day old, Marconi suggested that it would be a useful public service to have a regular time signal provided by the Greenwich Observatory. This suggestion was met with a deafening silence at first. This may be because the British Broadcasting Company (it was not yet a Corporation in those days) already broadcast a regular time signal before the seven o'clock and nine o'clock evening news bulletins. However, it was perhaps a little basic compared to the technology that was to follow: the duty announcer, who had a piano to hand (as one does!), would strike up the Westminster Chimes. Then, the piano was replaced with a set of tubular bells, which were installed in the Continuity Studio. (This was long before Mike Oldfield's 1973 album Tubular Bells was released.) They were used to great effect and proved to be a very popular event for those listening in.

As is always the case in these matters, somebody soon has a *'bright idea.'* On this occasion, the idea was to bring in some master clocks that controlled 'slave' clocks in all the studios. Wherever you went, if you should glance up at a clock, it would be – as it were – 'singing from the same song sheet' as all the others. Apparently (this was all long before my time) the system emitted a *tick* that was the cue for the announcer to count himself towards the hour so that he could strike a gong exactly on the hour. Touch of J. Arthur Rank here. History doesn't relate if the ticks were heard by the listener, and one has to presume that the announcer didn't do his countdown out loud.

In 1923, Frank Hope-Jones, the well-known amateur radio enthusiast and horologist, had just finished giving a talk on his favourite subject, and, being a stickler for time, counted the remaining five seconds up to 2200 hours out loud. His suggestion after the broadcast was that perhaps the BBC might find a way of producing an accurately-timed countdown to the hour. The first General Manager of the BBC, John Reith – later to be the first Director-General – got in a huddle with the then Astronomer Royal Sir Frank Watson Dyson to discuss this suggestion. The outcome was that a couple of modified clocks were used by the Observatory to emit time signals. The necessary modifications cost £20 per clock. Just before the allotted time, a 1kHz oscillator generated six short pips, the first of which was five seconds before the allotted time, which meant that the last pip signified the allotted time precisely. These Pips had to travel down an ordinary telephone line to Broadcasting House. Thus was the birth of the Pips on February 5th, 1924 at 2130.

Thus it remained until 13 years later the BBC had a rather surprising item of mail. A letter from the Admiralty Secretary suggested that, as no charge had been made for providing this service to the BBC, it was high time that a fee was levied, and thenceforward £520 per annum was to be charged for supplying the Pips. It is here that you discover that the BBC was governed by the Navy – or so it seemed.

The then Deputy Director-General, Vice-Admiral Sir Charles Carpendale, was not at all happy about this, so asked his colleagues to come up with a list of services that the BBC supplied to the Admiralty at no charge. A game of 'tit-for-tat' was in the making. The list that was put forward was quite impressive. It included announcing the departure and arrival of His Majesty's ships, weather forecasts, gale warnings, and the current vacancies for naval cadets in the Royal Navy College Dartmouth. A fair amount of bluster ensued as the Admiralty feared that they could be in for a sizeable bill. In fact, under the BBC Charter, the Corporation was 'obliged' to provide such services to everyone without cost – which remains the case today. But the point had been made, so some horse trading was done, the Admiralty bill was never paid, honour was satisfied, and the quid pro quo continued.

In 1957, pantechnicons arrived at Greenwich to move the Royal Observatory down to Herstmonceux in Sussex. This was a time of change – one of many to come. Electronic clocks now ruled the day. Two high-quality telephone lines were rented permanently, running from Sussex to Broadcasting House, which made the whole service of generating and providing the Pips a much more reliable operation. There was the odd occasion when the system spat out an unwanted pip in the middle of a programme, and for one reason and another this has tended to continue from time to time, but it has more to do with human failings than technical ones. So, the Pips had a new home in the depths of the lush Sussex countryside, linked to the GMT reference clocks.

With the introduction in 1972 of UTC (as mentioned above), all broadcast time signals from that year onwards were synchronized with International Atomic Time. However, the leap seconds play havoc with the Pips as a seventh pip is required every now and again! Oh dear, how do we know which pip actually signifies the hour? Fortunately someone had the bright idea of lengthening the final pip, the one that signifies the hour, so even when there is an extra (short) pip slipped in at 2359 and 60 seconds for a leap second, everyone knows that 0000 is the start of the longer final pip.

But we are not done yet. Towards the end of the 1980s there were more changes at the RGO (Royal Greenwich Observatory). Shock horror, the BBC was informed that the RGO would cease to provide the Pips. Time now for the BBC boffins to come up with a replacement system that would not only sound the same but be just as accurate. Some very sophisticated time equipment was duly designed and built. At its heart is an extremely accurate clock that constantly compared itself to all other time references the world over, including the GPS (Global Positioning Satellite Navigation System), which many of us use in our cars these days.

Just a few years ago, in 2006, the BBC Pips needed to relocate once again, due to a major redevelopment of the central London site that included three buildings being demolished and a total refurbishment of the original Broadcasting House. The opportunity was taken to replace the system with a new version very like the previous one. Maybe that will be it for a while now? Well, yes and no. I think the Pips generation system will probably stay in place for a good long while now but there was yet another problem that needed sorting out. This was to do with the dreaded digital factor, not to mention listening to the radio on the Internet. I am talking about delays here, which can and do become annoyingly noticeable. Once again I will not go into the technical complexities of all this. Suffice to say that whether you prefer the sound quality of Digital Audio Broadcasting (DAB) or not – and my jury is still out on that one – it takes time to convert the audio into a digital format and spurt it off to the transmitters, where it once again has to be converted back into audio. On top of that, if you listen to audio off the BBC website, a further block of time is needed for the passage of those signals through space, time, Dr Who's Tardis and goodness knows what else, and yet further conversions are executed that may well involve satellites. The difference in this instance could amount to as much as 10 seconds or perhaps even more. To try and smooth all this out though in a completely artificial way, the Pips are delayed so that they *appear* to be on time. It's all down to smoke and mirrors, but I suppose if it *sounds* OK, never fret too much at how it is achieved. I do feel sorry for someone being interviewed on radio or TV though, when a question is asked and clearly that question doesn't reach the interviewee for several seconds. Meanwhile you pop out into the kitchen to make some tea or finish the crossword while you wait for this turgid exercise to be completed. It really does get in the way of smooth-running programmes. I frequently curse it roundly, not least when somebody claims it is 'progress.'

So there we are, we've messed about with time so much that although you think it's today it might really be next Tuesday. It could be quite an adventure finding out. Good luck.

Right, so I hope we have got our heads round GMT, but that is not all that is famous about Greenwich. The first Tudor king, Henry VII, built a palace there, which reputedly was his favourite. His son Henry VIII was born there, and held two of his six weddings there – to Catherine of Aragon and to Anne of Cleves. Henry VIII's two daughters, Mary and Elizabeth, were also born there, and his son Edward VI was to die there in 1553. Henry VIII chose Deptford and Woolwich as the locations for his royal dockyards as they were close to Greenwich Palace. During Elizabeth I's reign, the Queen used the palace for festivals and 'launch parties' to send off many of that era's great voyages of exploration. Towards the end of her reign, a trust was set up that was later to finance the Royal Hospital for Seamen, a charitable trust to take care of seamen disabled during naval campaigns. The hospital building was in fact constructed on the site of the old Tudor palace, to a design by Sir Christopher Wren. Building began in 1696, and the first naval pensioners arrived a decade later. They were provided with beds rather than the hammocks they had been used to, but their diet was not so dissimilar, comprising bread, beer and boiled meat. During the 19th century the number of eligible pensioners fell away. Britain really did rule the waves in the Victorian era, but the Navy was less busy, so there were fewer casualties to be taken care of. In the end the Hospital closed in 1869.

The next occupiers, the Royal Naval College, used the site as a naval training centre for preparing officers from all over the world for command. The Royal Naval Museum was also established here, along with the Naval Gallery, which both stayed in Greenwich until they were transferred to the National Maritime Museum in 1936. Francis Chichester was knighted here by HM Queen Elizabeth II in 1967 after his solo circumnavigation of the globe in his boat *Gipsy Moth IV*. This was nearly 400 years after Francis Drake was knighted by Elizabeth I (on board the *Golden Hind* at nearby Deptford) for completing the first circumnavigation of the globe by an Englishman. The best touch of all was that the same sword was used for both dubbings. Technology had changed somewhat, but both those journeys were amazing feats of seamanship. Even though the first was completed with a full crew and Francis Chichester completed his circumnavigation single-handed, the odds against both men, in different ways, were huge. *Gipsy Moth IV* is displayed today alongside the *Cutty Sark* at Greenwich.

And what of the *Cutty Sark*, that famous old nautical lady? First of all, why is she so called? What is a cutty sark, apart from a delicious and well known blend of Scotch whisky? It means 'chemise' or 'undergarment' in Scotland, and got Robert Burns quite excited in his comic poem *Tam o'Shanter*, where Nannie Dee was dancing in her linen 'cutty sark', which was given her as a child but in adulthood was a wee bit small and apparently rather erotic to observe. The *Cutty Sark* was built in 1869 as a tea clipper, the type of fast sailing ship that sailed to China and then raced back to England laden with tea. If you came back ahead of the others with the first tea of the year, there were handsome bonuses to be earned (the tea trade at that time was a very popular and profitable business to be in).

The development of reliable steamships, and the opening of the Suez Canal, shortened the journey-time, and the clippers eventually could no longer compete, although it has to be said that the *Cutty Sark* was able to outrun some of the steamers. When she retired from the tea trade, she switched to the Australian wool trade and she made some record-breaking runs to and from the other side of the world. She went on to have a motley career, and was sold again in 1922, ending up as a stationary training ship in Kent, after her new owner had spent much time and money restoring her to her original appearance. Much later, and by now in need of further restoration work, she was towed into a specially-made dry dock at Greenwich in 1954 where she has remained ever since. She has been visited by millions of people, but the wear and tear over the years necessitated further work. This began in 2006, but disaster struck her the following year while still being restored: very early one May morning a fire broke out, causing a huge amount of damage. Luckily about 50% of her superstructure had previously been removed to be treated elsewhere, including her famous figurehead, the masts and rigging, the coach house and most of the decking. So, bad though the fire was, the damage was more limited than might have been the case.

It is hoped that she will be fully repaired and restored by the time the 2012 Olympics take place: the huge influx of visitors to London and specifically to Greenwich that year may generate the revenue needed to pay for all the work to be carried out. The Heritage Lottery Fund provided about £10 million originally but the fire increased costs, bringing the sum required up to some £23 million.

So, as you have now discovered, Greenwich has and still does have a large part to play in Britain's naval history, and will probably continue to do so for many more years to come.

FOURTEEN

—

A LIFE ON THE
OCEAN WAVE

We are nearing the end of this history of the waters around our shores, inspired by the BBC Radio 4 Shipping Forecasts. I have to admit that I didn't envisage, when I started writing this book, that the subject matter would broaden to take in so many events and wildly differing subjects in our history.

If we had been a landlocked country, our history would have been so very different and probably nothing like as interesting, colourful or exciting. But for the card that nature dealt us, quite apart from anything else, there would quite simply not have been the need for the Shipping Forecast. This means of telling ships what is in store came about through the ingenuity of clever, talented and far-sighted people, who saw that they had the means of making the lives of others safer and easier, and went to great lengths to make sure that others benefited from their ability, at times when perhaps the answers lay only in their hands. Since its conception, it has evolved over the decades into a cultural treasure of our nation – so much more than just the hard facts in its prose. It is left for us all to marvel at the attraction this all-encompassing litany holds for people of all ages and backgrounds who have no connection with the sea or ships. And marvel we probably will, for all time. Well, if not for all time, then certainly for quite a while anyway.

What of the future of the Shipping Forecast as a broadcast fixture in the Radio 4 schedule? Will it continue, will it need to continue, or will the relentless tidal swirl of technology finally wash it away? How dare I suggest such a thing: it brings a very whiff of treason to the air. Radio 4 listeners – of whom I am one – will flare their nostrils, reach for their quills and green ink. They will tap away at their computers, writing letters to *The Times* and *Daily Telegraph* in the strongest possible terms at their command, forbidding such a notion from occurring, not only in their lifetime, but ever. Mark Damazer, the previous Controller of Radio 4, probably feared for his very existence when such a proposition was suggested to him. He probably envisioned himself hung from the highest yardarm, after being flogged with a cat o'nine tails before being urged along the gangplank to a sure demise in the deep blue sea below. He was quoted as saying that the forecast was baffling, yet it scans poetically, it has got a rhythm of its own, and it is both eccentric and unique – it is very English. Those alone are good enough reasons for leaving it where it is, even if it does baffle some. A little bafflement never did anyone any harm. The present Controller, Gwyneth Williams, who took over the reins at Radio 4 in October 2010, has this to say on the subject:

"The Shipping Forecast, which has been on Radio 4 for as long as I can remember, transports us through its cadences to a place where the elements and the sea and a journey are what matter, in contrast to the treadmill of most of our lives."

The future practicalities, the endless siren call for bigger cuts in expenditure, for greater economy in everything that everyone does, no matter where, no matter what, might be the one thing that finally 'does for' the forecasts. I am not the prophet of doom, I can only guess at what might happen at some point in the future. Regardless of its broadcast form, the Shipping Forecast will certainly continue to be relayed by a variety of means to those who really need it to protect them and their livelihoods. In addition to the Radio 4 broadcasts, you can already get the forecasts on local radio and TV, newspapers, websites, Coastguard stations via VHF/FM radio, on Navtex and on mobile phone via voicemail or text. However, for those of you who are seafarers and do rely on the Shipping Forecast on Radio 4 – like my friend and former Radio 4 colleague Carolyn Brown – help remains at hand. She says she has spent many a long night wedged in a soggy cockpit, with her radio jammed between her knees, torch held between her teeth, waiting with pencil and paper in hand for the strains of *Sailing By* followed by the Shipping Forecast to help speed her on her way. Listen in and listen on. For those of you who are not seafarers but listen to the forecast purely because it's there, while you are in the safety and protective weatherproofed comfort of your home – listen in and listen on. The Shipping Forecast must prevail: it has earned its place in our heritage.

While we have people who just like to go out for a sail; while we have people who come and go on trips of adventure; while we need imports and exports ferried around the world on cargo ships; while we not only need but want to use the waters around our coasts, there will always be the Shipping Forecasts to aid those on the high seas, speeding them on their way as safely as possible.

As we bob up and down surrounded by the North Sea, the English Channel, the Irish Sea and indeed the Atlantic, the title of this chapter comes to mind. *A Life on the Ocean Wave* is the first line of a song composed by Henry Russell, way back in 1838. The song's lyrics came from a poem that his friend Epes Sargent had been inspired to write on an occasion when the two men were walking in Battery Park in New York and stopped to watch the ships sailing into New York Harbour. The end result, of the poem being set to music, proved very popular in both England and the USA. In 1882 a man with the grand title of Deputy Adjutant-General of the Royal Marines asked that each of the three Royal Marine Divisions, in Portsmouth, Plymouth and Chatham, put forward an arrangement for a new regimental march, preferably based on a naval song. The bandmaster from Chatham submitted a quick march based mainly on Russell's song, but with a short central section from *The Sea* by Sigismund Neukomm. This entry was the one chosen by the War Office to be the regimental march of the Corps, subsequently being authorised by the Admiralty in 1920, and it has remained so ever since. When I was a small boy in Deal I often heard this march coming from the Royal Marines School of Music. It has four verses and finishes with the lines:

And the song of our hearts shall be
While the wind and water rave
A life on the heaving sea
A home on the bounding wave.

The march was just as popular in the USA as here, and it is also the official march of the US Merchant Marine Academy.

As I write this page the third generation of Cunard's cruise liner, *Queen Elizabeth*, has arrived in Southampton to be named by Her Majesty the Queen on October 11th, 2010. The first was named after the present Queen's mother, the late Queen Elizabeth The Queen Mother, in 1938. The *Queen Elizabeth* retired in 1968 ahead of the launch of the *Queen Elizabeth 2* in 1969. The 'QE2' was the Cunard flagship ocean liner for 35 years, and was retired fully from service for Cunard in 2008. The new *Queen Elizabeth*, will be making her maiden voyage to the Canary Islands the day after the naming ceremony. Aboard her will be all the latest technology to aid her through weather fair and foul, and on the return leg of the trip I'm sure there will be a radio set tuned to BBC Radio 4 long wave somewhere on the bridge. This will pick up the Shipping Forecasts as she sails into the western approaches to the British Isles, just as a final check that relatively smooth waters await her as she glides into Southampton Docks.

Meanwhile, back in Portland Place, the good ship Broadcasting House clad in its white Portland stone sits becalmed, facing south towards Oxford Circus. Messrs Prospero and Ariel stand guard over her front door in perpetuity. It was thought an apt choice, inspired by William Shakespeare's play *The Tempest*, as Prospero was a magician and Ariel a spirit of the air, through which radio waves travel. What better way was there to represent the BBC, when it first moved into its headquarters, than to take inspiration from one of the Bard's better-known plays?

So there we have it, an inextricable link between the BBC and the high seas and the subject which started this all off – the Shipping Forecast.

FIFTEEN

—

A FINAL NOTE

A year has already passed since I was last in the Radio 4 Continuity Studio, a place that had become my second home over several decades working for the BBC, both on the staff and as a freelancer. So there I was late one September night in 2009 – for the very last time. It felt strange knowing that these last few hours leading up to 0100 were to be the final ones for me in my oasis of tranquillity.

In came the Shipping Forecast by email at about 2330. I made sure it was the correct one, and that it was all there. It was. Just over an hour later, with the studio lights dimmed just the way I liked them for this time of day, imagining a similar level of light for those who would be listening at home, *Sailing By* ended and off I went with the words *"And now here's the Shipping Forecast…"*

Those last 11 minutes of my career with the BBC went by alarmingly quickly. Before I knew it, I heard myself saying:

> *"And that ends the Shipping Bulletin and also brings to an end our programmes today on Radio 4. In a few moments we join the BBC World Service. This is Peter Jefferson wishing you on behalf*

of everyone here on Radio 4 a very peaceful night… Good night."

I then played in the National Anthem, faded up the Pips and the World Service, and sat back heavily in my chair, both with relief that all had gone according to plan, and with the sudden realisation that I would never again be doing this. Some sadness, of course, and many great friends I would miss working with. A chapter had ended, a window had closed, but I knew that somewhere at some point a door would open – and a few months later a door did open, and what you have just read was the result.

GLOSSARY

Back Timing	Counting backwards from finishing point
BBC	British Broadcasting Corporation (British Broadcasting Company Ltd prior to 1927)
BST	British Summer Time
Cart Player	Cartridge Player
CW	Continuous Wave
DAB	Digital Audio Broadcasting
DGPS	Digital Global Positioning System
DSC	Digital Selective Calling
EPIRB	Emergency Position Indicating Radio Beacon
FM	Frequency Modulation
GLA	General Lighthouse Authority
GMDSS	Global Maritime Distress Safety System
GMT	Greenwich Mean Time
GPO	General Post Office
GPS	Global Positioning System
GTS	Greenwich Time Signal
HM	His/Her Majesty('s)
HMNB	His/Her Majesty's Naval Base
HMS	His/Her Majesty's Ship
HMY	His/Her Majesty's Yacht
HQ	Headquarters
IERS	International Earth Rotation Service
LF	Low Frequency
LW	Long Wave
MCA	Maritime and Coastguard Agency
Met Office	The Meteorological Office
MF	Medium Frequency
Mic	Microphone
MOD	Ministry of Defence
MSC	Mediterranean Shipping Company

MV............................ Motor Vessel
NATO...................... North Atlantic Treaty Organization
Navtex.................... Navigational Telex
NLB.......................... Northern Lighthouse Board
RAF.......................... Royal Air Force
RGO......................... Royal Greenwich Observatory
RN............................ Royal Navy
RNAD...................... Royal Naval Armaments Depot
RNAS...................... Royal Naval Air Service
RNLI........................ Royal National Lifeboat Institution
RORO...................... Roll-On/Roll-Off
RRS.......................... Royal Research Ship
Sat nav.................... Satellite Navigation
SI derived unit...... Unit of measurement derived from the seven
                          base units in the International System of Units
SIS/M16.................. Secret Intelligence Service
SM............................ Studio Manager
SS............................. Steamship
UFO.......................... Unidentified Flying Object
UNHCR.................. United Nations High Commissioner
                          for Refugees
USS.......................... Unites States Ship
UT............................ Universal Time
VHF.......................... Very High Frequency

SOURCES & FURTHER READING

BOOKS, POETRY & LYRICS

Adams, Martin. *The Shipping Forecast* poem, Wolf Magazine 2004

Barker, Les. *Cats For The Blind*, Songs and Poems of Les Barker

Binge, Ronald. *Sailing By – A tune on the ocean of sound*

Blur, *This is a Low*, words and music by Damon Albarn and
Graham Coxon and Steven Alexander James and David Rowntree
© 1998, reproduced by permission of EMI Music Publishing Ltd,
London W8 5SW

Briggs, A, *History of Broadcasting in the United Kingdom* from The
Golden Age of Wireless (1995, Oxford University Press)
Bruce, Ken. *The Radio Companion*, 1991

Clarke, Gillian. *Farewell Finisterre* from *A Recipe For Water*,
Carcanet 2009

Crandall, J. *Vikings, Longboats and Navigation* (2006) from *Ancestral
Nautical Knowledge*

Darling, Julia. *Forecasting*, Sauce 1994, by The Poetry Virgins from
Diamond Twig, Newcastle

Duffy, Carol Ann. *Prayer* from *Mean Time*, Anvil 1993

Heaney, Seamus. The Shipping Forecast, Faber & Faber 2010

Hewittt & Jacques. *A Life on the Ocean Wave* 1838, words E. Sargent and music H. Russell

Marine Observer, pp. Vol, 1 pp. 50-52 (1924) from the *Encyclopaedia Britannica & National Dictionary of Biography*

Radiohead. *In Limbo* (Yorke / Greenwood / Greenwood / Selway / O'Brien), Warner / Chappell Music Ltd

Shutt, R.T. *A Wedding Forecast* (2002) R. T. Shutt, St. Mary's Church, Send, Surrey, UK

Street, Sean. *Shipping Forecast, Donegal* from *Time Between Tides – New and Selected Poems 1980 – 2009*, Rockingham Press 2009

Woodroffe, A. *Fastnet Storm – a Forecaster's viewpoint* from *The Meteorological Magazine*, No. 1311, Vol. 110, Met Office, October 1981

Winton, J. *Recollections of the Falklands Campaign from Captain Michael Layard RN, CM, Senior Naval Officer SS Atlantic Conveyor* from *Signals from the Falklands: the Navy in the Falklands conflict: an anthology of personal experience*, Leo Cooper 1995

All meteorology information, shipping forecast maps, and the diagrams of cones in Chapter Eight, were retrieved from the National Meteorological Library and Archive and are based on Crown Copyright Data.

WEB SITES THAT MAY BE OF INTEREST

Air Ministry Roof
www.britishpathe.com / record.php?id=6

Battle of the Atlantic
www.bbc.co.uk/history/worldwars/wwtwo/battle_atlantic_
01.shtml

Battle of Dogger Bank (1915)
www.naval-history.net/

Battle of Jutland
www.tripatlas.com/Battle_of_Jutland

Battle of the Atlantic
www.bbc.co.uk/history/worldwars/wwtwo/battle_atlantic_
01.shtml

Bay of Biscay
weather.mailasail.com/Franks-Weather/Crossing-Biscay-
Meteorologists-Advice

BBC Radio
www.radio-electronics.com/info/radio_history/index.php

Beaufort, Sir Francis
www.pgil-eirdata.org/html/pgil_datasets/authors/b/
Beaufort,F/life.htm
irishscientists.tripod.com/scientists/FRANCIS.HTM

Beaufort Scale, The, Fact Sheet No 6 (2007)
www.metoffice.gov.uk/corporate/library/factsheets/factsheet06.pdf

Bell Rock Lighthouse, Who Built the? (2009) C. Spencer
www.bbc.co.uk/history/british/empire_seapower/bell_rock_
01.shtml

British Summer Time (2009) ROG learning team
www.nmm.ac.uk/explore/astronomy-and-time/time-facts/
british-summer-time

Candle Power from Dictionary of Units of Measurement,
R. Rowlett
www.unc.edu/~rowlett/units/dictC.html

Cargo ship sinks with 2800 cars (2002)
news.scotsman.com/englishchannelcollisions/Cargo-ship-sinks-
with-2800.2386502.jp

Channel Tunnel
www.eurotunnel.com/ukcP3Main/ukcCorporate/
ukcTunnelInfrastructure/ukcDevelopment/ukpHistory

Chichester, Francis
www.BBC.co.uk/devon/discovering/famous/francis_chichester.
html

**Climate variability and ecosystem response in the German
Bight**, M. H. Schlüter
w3k.gkss.de/staff/storch/pdf/schlueter.0708.ODfinal.pdf

Clyde, HMNB
www.Scottish-places.info/features.html

Cod Wars
www.britains-smallwars.com/RRGP/CodWar.htm

Cromarty
www.black-isle.info/Cromarty/
www.secretsofscotland.org.uk

worldportsource.com/ports/GBR

Cutty Sark – Clipper Ship
cuttysark.com

Cutty Sark (2010)
www.cuttysark.org.uk/index.cfm?fa=contentGeneric.
fdvmyqknhxemnmvz

Dandy (1998)
www.mondofacto.com/facts/dictionary?query=dandy&action=l
ook+it+up

Dogger Bank
hullwebs.co.uk/disaster/dogger-bank/voyage-of-the-damned.
html

Dover
www.dover-kent.co.uk/history/cinque_ports.htm

Dover Castle, History
www.dover-kent.co.uk/defence/castle_history.htm
historickent.com/dovcast.html

Earl of Sandwich and the Origin of the Sandwich
www.open-sandwich.co.uk/town_history/sandwich_origin.htm

Eddystone Lighthouse History (2005)
www.eddystoneeel.com/

English Channel ferry warning as ships collide (2002) J. McBeth
news.scotsman.com/englishchannelcollisions/English-Channel-
ferry-warning-as.2386971.jp

English Lighthouse beams out Shipping Forecast from BBC From Our Own Correspondent (2010) Z. Soanes
news.bbc.co.uk/1/hi/programmes/from_our_own_
correspondent/8622292.stm

Fair Isle
www.fairisle.org.uk/

Fastnet Race 1979
www.seayourhistory.org.uk/content/view/598/767/

FitzRoy, Robert (Admiral)
www.admiralfitzroy.co.uk/
www.users.zetnet.co.uk/tempusfugit/marine/notes.htm

FitzRoy barometers
www.sciencemuseum.org.uk/onlinestuff/stories/heavy_weather.
aspx?page=2

Forth
www.grantonhistory.org
www.royal-navy.org

Forties Oil Field
scotlandonsunday.scotsman.com/spectrum

German Bight Coast
www.floodsite.net/html/pilot_site_germanbight.htm

Giant 'super river' carved English Channel 450,000 years ago
(2009, November 30th) ANI
www.dnaindia.com/scitech/report_giant-super-river-carved-
english-channel-450000-years-ago_1318404

Goodwin Sands, History
uk-shore.com/blog/2008/05/goodwin

Greenwich Mean Time
www.worldtimezones.com/guides/greenwich_mean-time

Greenwich Time Signal (2008) M. Todd
www.miketodd.net/other/gts.htm

Greenwich Palace
www.oldroyalnavalcollege.org/greenwich-palace

Heavy Weather
www.sciencemuseum.org.uk/onlinestuff/stories/heavy_
weather.aspx

Herald of Free Enterprise, MS
www.dover-kent.co.uk/transport/herald_disaster.htm

Historic Vessels At Risk from L.V. (1903) **Juno Light Vessel**
www.transportbritain.co.uk/index.html

Horatio Nelson, 1st Viscount Nelson
www.historyofwar.org/

Humber Lifeboat Station
www.rnli.org.uk/rnli_near_you/north/stations/

Humber East Yorkshire
Humber, River
www.riverhumber.com

Near-miss for wreck (2002) Innes, J
news.scotsman.com/englishchannelcollisions/Nearmiss-for-wreck.2387394.jp

Iolaire, HMS
www.c-e-n.org/iolair.html

Isle of Portland
www.iknow-dorset.co.uk

Light Vessel No 72 (1996, February 13th)
www.nationalhistoricships.org.uk/ships_register.
php?action=ship&id=143

Lighthouse For Sale: Squatter Included (2008, March 14th)
S. Clark
lighthouse-news.com/2008/03/14/lighthouse-for-sale-squatter-included/

Lighthouse painted pink with yellow spots (2001, February 9th)
news.bbc.co.uk/1/hi/scotland/1162552.stm

Lighthouses face uncertain future (2010, January 29th) K. Dawson
news.bbc.co.uk/1/hi/england/8471030.stm

Lizard Lighthouse
www.photographers-resource.co.uk/A_heritage/Lighthouses/
LG2_EW/Lizard_Lighthouse.htm

Mackerel war, Why is Britain braced for a? (2010) A. McFarlane
www.bbc.co.uk/news/magazine-11062674

Margate Harbour (1980)

margate.org.uk/index.php?page=margaet-harbour-1980

Margate Pier – 1953 Storm Damage

www.thanetarch.co.uk/Virtual%20Museum/3_Displays/G10%20
Displays/Margate%20Pier%201953%20Storm%20Damage.html

Mary Rose: A Great Ship of Henry VIII, A. Lambert

www.bbc.co.uk/history/british/tudors/mary_rose_01.shtml

MCA

www.mcga.gov.uk/c4mca/mcga07-home

Met Office History

www.metoffice.gov.uk/about-us/who/our-history

Met Office A short history of Forecasting for Mariners

www.exetermemories.co.uk/em/_commercial/metoffice.php

MI6 boss Sir John Scarlett still signs letters in green ink (2009,
July 27th) M. Moore

www.telegraph.co.uk/news/uknews/law-and-order/5918467/
MI6-boss-Sir-John-Scarlett-still-signs-letters-in-green-ink.html

Ministry of Defence, History

www.mod.uk/DefenceInternet/AboutDefence/History/

Mumbles Lighthouse

www.trinityhouse.co.uk/interactive/gallery/mumbles.html

Napoli, MSC: Timeline (2008, October)

www.bbc.co.uk/devon/content/articles/2007/07/16/napoli_
timeline_feature.shtml

National Meteorological Library and Archive
www.metoffice.gov.uk/corporate/library

National Severe Weather Warning Service (2010)
weatherfaqs.org.uk/node/176

Naval Battles
www.information-britain.co.uk/famdates.php?id=1055

Navigation Lights (2010)
Knol.google.com/k/karl/navigation-lights/3dukx1f6hofh4/1

Plymouth's proud naval history, L. Joint from **Devon Local History**
news.bbc.co.uk/local/devon/hi/people_and_places/history/
newsid_8278000/8278316.stm

Port Lynas lighthouse for sale at £1.5m (2010)
www.bbc.co.uk/news/uk-wales-10777054

Port and Starboard Origin
www.harbourguides.com/news.php/PORT-AND-
STARBOARD-ORIGIN

Portsmouth Royal Dockyard History
www.portsmouthdockyard.org.uk/Page%203.htm

Posh
thesaurus.com/browse/posh

Project Redsand
www.project-redsand.com/books.htm

Quality Handbook Annex: WGSSDS-Celtic Sea Sole (2004)
www.ices.dk/reports/ACFM/2004/WGSSDS/Quality%20
Handbook%20-%20Celtic%20Sea%20Sole.pdf

Queen Elizabeth II cruise liner (2010)
www.bbc.co.uk/news/uk-england-hampshire-11156271

Radio 4, a listener's guide (2006)
www.kuro5hin.org/story/2006/9/4/22167/17993

Rent a Lighthouse, Rural Retreats
101shortbreaks.co.uk/lighthouses-to-rent/

Robert Farnon Society (2004) M. Carey
www.rfsoc.org.uk/rbinge.shtml

Robert FitzRoy , 1805–1865 (2005)
www.bbc.co.uk/dna/h2g2/A2344736

Rockall
www.bbc.co.uk/dna/h2g2/A755 787

Rockall (2002) Woodpigeon
www.bbc.co.uk/dna/h2g2/alabaster/A755787

Royal Hospital for Seamen
www.oldroyalnavalcollege.org/royal-hospital-for-seamen,
27,AT.html

Royal Marines. The Regimental Marches of Her Majesty's Royal Marines
www.royalmarinesbands.co.uk/reference/FS_reg_march.htm

Royal Navy Customs and Traditions, C. V. Fisher
www.hmsrichmond.org/avast/customs.htm

Navy, History of the, from **A Few Naval Customs, Expressions, Traditions and Superstitions,** (Gieves) Captain W.N.T Beckett MVO, DSC, RN
www.exeterflotilla.org/history_misc/nav_customs/nc_home.html

Salvage of luxury car cargo ship delayed (2002) J. Innes
news.scotsman.com/englishchannelcollisions/Salvage-of-luxury-car-cargo.2386836.jp

Sandwich People and History: Ian Fleming
www.open-sandwich.co.uk/town_history/scrapbook/ian_fleming.htm

Scapa Flow
gouk.about.com/od/travelbyinterest/qt/ScapaFlow.htmShipping Forecast

Shipbuilding in the North East
www.bbc.co.uk/nationonfilm/topics/ship-building/background.shtml

Shipping Forecast
www.metoffice.gov.uk/weather/marine/shipping_forecast.html

Shipping Forecast, The, Fact Sheet No 8 (2007)
www.metoffice.gov.uk/corporate/library/factsheets/factsheet08.pdf

Shipping Forecast (2010)
www.bbc.co.uk/weather/coast/shipping/index.shtml

Shipping Forecast's 'baffling' legacy (2007) **K. Utsire, North & South**
www.newsbiscuit.com/2010/04/16/on-going-conflict-between-north-and-south-utsire-could-end-shipping-forecast

Shipping Forecast, Terminology in the
weatherfaqs.org.uk/book/export/html/78

Shipwrecks of Lundy (2007) P. Robson
www.lundypete.com/wrecks.htm

SIS or MI6. What's in a name? (2005)
www.sis.gov.uk/our-history/sis-or-mi6.html

SIS, History
www.sis.gov.uk/our-history.html

Southampton, History
www.visit-southampton.co.uk/site/research-zone/history-of-southampton

Southampton Water
visit-southampton.co.uk/site/research-zone/historyofsouthampton

Statutory Instrument 1989 No. 1295, HM Government
www.legislation.gov.uk/uksi/1989/1295/contents/made

Stevenson, Robert
www.bellrock.org.uk/stevensons/

Sussex Coastline, The Ever Changing
www.westsussex.info/sussex-coastline.shtml

Trinity House (2010)
www.trinityhouse.co.uk/about_us/history/index

Trinity House Lighthouse Service (2010)
www.trinityhouse.co.uk/about_us/what_we_do/gla.html

Trinity House Lighthouses (2010)
www.trinityhouse.co.uk/aids_to_navigation/the_task/
lighthouses.html

How does a Barometer Measure Air Pressure? Warboys, J
weather.about.com/od/weatherinstruments/a/barometers.
htm?p=1

New Submarine in a class of its own (2010) Wyatt, C
www.bbc.co.uk/news/uk-11173266

Viking
www.answers.com/topic/viking-31

Viking Ship buried beneath pub (2007)
news.bbc.co.uk/1/hi/england/merseyside/6986986.stm

Vikings
www.infobritain.co.uk/Viking_History.htm

Vintage Norton Motorcycles (2010) J. D. Kruif
http://rapidhare.blogspot.com/

Walmer Lifeboat Station
www.rnli.org.uk/rnli_near_you/east/stations/walmerkent

War at Sea, The: 1914-1918 (2009) Dr E. Grove
www.bbc.co.uk/history/worldwars/wwone/war_sea_
gallery_08.shtml

Weather – Beaufort Scale, Forecasts (2009)
www.btinternet.com/~keith.bater/forecasts_weather_sea.htm

White Cliffs of Dover Sale (2010) V. Allen
www.dailymail.co.uk/news/article-1249194/Dover-symbol-
British-sovereignty

Wireless Telegraphy
www.mhs.ox.ac.uk/marconi/collection/glossary

Wreckers, The (2007) B. Bathhurst
www.open2.net/timewatch/2008/wreckers.html

Zeebrugge Raid
www.firstworldwar.com/.htm

INDEX

A

Agincourt, Battle of 124
Air Ministry 26, 45
Ambush, HMS 144
American Apache Corporation 98
American War of Independence 104
Amethyst, HMS 185
Ardanamurchan Lighthouse, see Lighthouses
Ariel 220
Arran, Isle of 172
Artful, HMS 144
Astute, HMS 144

B

Bailey, see Shipping Areas
Barometer, see Meteorological
Battery Park 219
Beachy Head Lighthouse, see Lighthouses
Beacons, see Meteorological
Beagle, HMS 24, 36–37, 59
Beatty, Admiral 98
Beaufort, Francis 36, 57–63
Beaufort Scale, see Meteorological
Beaufort Wind Scale, see Meteorological
Bell Rock Lighthouse, see Lighthouses
Benbecula 33, 144
Binge, Ronald 20, 81–83
Biscay, Bay of, see Shipping Areas

Bismarck 113, 152–153

Black, Jim 83

Blacknore Point Lighthouse, see Lighthouses

Blériot, Louis 112

BLT 116

Boadicea 23

Bonner, Charles 174

Bracknell, see Meteorological

Britannia, Royal Yacht 125

British Isles 25, 28, 37, 41, 73, 95–96, 102, 107, 111, 121, 143, 145,
      155, 156, 159, 169, 220

British Telecom 25

Broadcasting

    British Broadcasting Company, the 28, 208, 224

    British Broadcasting Corporation, the 28, 224

    Digital Audio Broadcasting 211, 224

    Pips 20, 49, 85, 208–212, 222

    Radio 4 16, 18, 28, 47, 48, 49, 72, 73, 74, 76, 83, 85, 89, 90, 91,
        216–218, 220, 221–222,

    Radio Caroline 120

    Radio transmitters 19, 47, 211

    Shipping Forecast, the 15–16, 20, 24, 47, 49, 56, 64–65, 74,
        76–79, 83, 86-87, 91, 132, 136, 138, 140, 144, 148, 183,
        216–220, 221–222

    Wireless 15, 26, 28, 177

Broadsword, HMS 139

Brown, Carolyn 218

BST, see Meteorological

Burns, Robert 214

C

Caesar, Julius, 23 111

Cap Gris Nez 110

Cape Wrath, Rattray Head 41–43

Carpathia 101

Carpendale, Sir Charles 210

Cart machines, see Meteorological

Catherine of Aragon 212

Chesapeake, USS. 141

Chichester, Sir Francis 213

Churchill, Sir Winston 115, 148

Cinque Ports 114–115

Clarke, Gillian 18, 71–72

Claudius, Emperor 112

Cleves, Anne of 212

Cliftonville Boarding School 109

Coastguard, HM 111

Cobra Mist, the 80

Cod Wars 147, 149–151

Commissioners of Irish Lights 157

Cones, see Meteorological

Corfield, Corrie 33

Corsewell, Lighthouse, see Lighthouses

Coulport, RNAD 144

Cromarty, see Shipping Areas

Cromwell, Oliver 126

Culdrose, RNAS 139

Cunard Atlantic Conveyor 154–155

Cutty Sark 213-215

D

Daily Mail, the 117
Daily Telegraph, the 217
Damazer, Mark 18, 74–75, 217
Darwin, Charles 24, 36, 59
Daventry, see Meteorological
D-Day 41, 45, 85, 124, 130
Deal 15, 118, 219
Deep Sea Pilotage Authority 157
Devonport, HMNB 130, 143, 153–154
Desborough Cut 96
Discovery, RSS 174
Dogger, see Shipping Areas
Donaldson, Peter 91
Dover, see Shipping Areas
Drake, Sir Francis 129
Dreadnought, HMS 126
Droitwich 19
Du Maurier, Daphne 165
Dubris 111, 160
Dubris Lighthouse, see Lighthouses
Duffy, Carol Ann 18, 69

E

Eddystone Lighthouse, see Lighthouses
Edgeworth, Honora 59
Eilean Mor, Lighthouse, see Lighthouses
Elizabeth I, Queen 157, 212–213
Emergency Position Indicating Radio Beacon, see Meteorological
English Channel 16, 94, 113–114, 121, 122, 126, 129, 140, 147, 218

Erika, Oil Tanker 132
Eugen, Prinz 113
Exploration of the Sea, ICES 151
Eyjafjallajökull, Volcano 149

F

Faeroes, see Shipping Areas
Fair Isle, see Shipping Areas
Falkland Islands, the 130, 154
Faslane 144
Fastnet, see Shipping Areas
Fastnet Race 137, 138–140
Finis terre 29
Finisterre, see Shipping Areas
Fisher, see Shipping Areas
Fitzroy, see Shipping Areas
FitzRoy, Robert 24, 36–39, 44, 134
Fleming, Ian 121
Fonnereau, Thomas 169
Forth, see Shipping Areas
Forties, see Shipping Areas
Fresnel, Augustine 164
Fry, Stephen 72

G

Gale warning(s) 25–26, 37, 47, 50, 51, 54, 56, 210
Gare du Nord 117
Gaul 111
General Electric, see Meteorological

General Lighthouse Authority, LGA, see Meteorological

General Post Office, see GPO

German Bight, see Shipping Areas

Gipsy Moth IV 213

Global Maritime Distress Safety System 179, 224

GMT, see Meteorological

Gneisenau 113

Golden Hind 213

Goodwin Sands 118, 120, 128

Goon Show, the 18

GPO 25–26, 224

Greenwich Mean Time, see Meteorological

Grogan, R T 152–153

Guardian, the 142

H

Hadrian, Emperor 24

Hartland Point, Lighthouse, see Lighthouses

Hayward, Jack 135–136

Heath, Sir Edward 139

Hebrides, see Shipping Areas

Heinkel 146

Heligoland, see Shipping Areas

Henry V, King 124

Henry VII, King 212

Henry VIII, King 124–125, 157, 212

Henry, Joseph 177

Herald of Free Enterprise, MS 127–128

Hermes, HMS 126

Herring fishing 33

Hitler, Adolph 100, 113

HMS, see individual ship name
Hood, HMS 100, 152–153, 185
Hope-Jones, Frank 209
Humber, see Shipping Areas

I

Ice Prince 168
Illustrious, HMS 126
Inshore Waters Forecast, see Meteorological
Inshore Waters Forecast map 43
International Earth Rotation Service, see Meteorological
Intrepid, HMS 126
Irish Sea, see Shipping Areas

J

Jamaica Inn 165
James I, King 157, 169
Jolly, Commander Richard 101
Junkers Ju 88, 100
Jutland, Battle of 97, 130

K

Keeler, Christine 174
Kent, HMS 126
Killigrew, Sir John 169
Kingsbury, Jimmy 28, 90

L

Landmark Trust, the 135 – 136
Layard, Sir Michael 153, 155
Lighthouses
    Ardnamurchan 175
    Beachy Head 170, 172
    Bell Rock 34 – 35, 160 – 161, 162, 164
    Blacknore Point 170
    Corsewell 172
    Dubris (Dover) 160
    Eddystone 160, 162 – 165
    Eilean Mor 175
    Hartland Point 135, 170
    Lizard 169–170
    Maryport 170
    Mumbles 168 – 169
    No Man's Land (Solent) Fort 173–174
    Orfordness 170
    Pharos 159 – 160
    Port Appin 176
    Port Lynas 173
    Lindbergh, Charles 178
    Lionheart, Richard the 202
    Lizard Lighthouse, see Lighthouses
    Lochalsh, Kyle of 145
    Long ship, Viking 95 – 97
Lundy, see Shipping Areas
Luftwaffe 100
Luray Victory 119

M

Macmillan, Harold 174

Malin, see Shipping Areas

Mantovani 82–83

Marconi, see Meteorological

Margate 109

Marine Differential Global Positioning System, see Meteorological

Maritime and Coastguard Agency, see Meteorological

Marsh, John 91

Mary Celeste 175

Mary Rose 124–126

Maryport, Lighthouse, see Lighthouses

Maunsell Sea Forts 98, 109

Mauretania 101

Mayflower 124

Melville, Herman 120–121

Menzies, Sir Robert 115

Metereological

    Barometer 38–39

    Beacons 120, 157–159, 177–179, 224

    Beaufort Scale 51, 62

    Beaufort Wind Scale Chart 57, 60–61

    Bracknell 45, 138, 140

    BST 56, 207, 224

    Cart machines 87

    Cones 37

    Daventry 19, 26

    Emergency Position Indicating Radio Beacon 179, 224

    General Electric 208

    General Lighthouse Authority, GLA 156, 158, 224

    GMT 204–212, 224

    Inshore Waters Forecast 41–43, 47, 49, 92

International Earth Rotation Service 206, 224
Marconi 208
Marine Differential Global Positioning System 159, 224
Maritime and Coastguard Agency 73, 127, 224
Met Office 24, 25, 30, 37, 40, 41, 44–47, 54, 72, 73, 88, 134, 224
Navtex 179, 218, 225
Semaphore 177
Signals 26–27
Supercomputers 45–46
Time 50–51, 56, 204–212
Ministry of Defence, the 45–46, 77–78, 79, 167, 173, 224
Moby Dick 120
MOD, see Ministry of Defence
Mohawk, HMS 101
Montagu, HMS 135
Morse Code 177–180
Morse, Samuel B 177
Mumbles Lighthouse, see Lighthouses
Music, see Sailing By

N

Napoleonic Wars 57, 129, 133, 141
Napoli, MSC 166–168
National Maritime Museum 213
National Trust 135–136
NATO 129, 150–151, 225
Navtex, see Meteorological
Nelson, Admiral Lord 125, 133
Neukomm, Sigismund 219
No Man's Land Lighthouse, see Lighthouses
Norge, SS 142, 145

Norland, RORO 154
North Eastern Victory 119
North, Ian 155
Northern Lighthouse Board 157, 160, 176, 225
North Utsire, see Shipping Areas
Norway 22, 33, 40, 113
Nove, C 91
Novello, Ivor 83

O

Oldfield, Mike 208
Orfordness, Lighthouse, see Lighthouses

P

Pas-de-Calais 110
Pharos 112
Pharos Lighthouse, see Lighthouses
Pheloung, Barrington 180
Piper Oil Field 99, 148
Plymouth, see Shipping Areas
Polar Star 136
Port Apin Lighthouse, see Lighthouses
Portland, see Shipping Areas
Port Lynas Lighthouse, see Lighthouses
Portsmen, the 114–115
Portsmouth, Harbour 122, 124–126, 173, 219
Portsmouth, HMNB 143
Posh 180
Prince of Wales, HMS 153

Prospero 220
Proulx, A. 72
Purdon, Iain 91

Q

QE2 129, 219
Queen Mother, the 115, 219

R

Redoutable 133
Reith, Lord John, 19 209
Rennie, John 160–161
RNLI 108, 118–119, 225
Rockall, see Shipping Areas
Roman Britain 23, 111–112, 122, 125, 128, 160
RORO ferry 127–128, 153–154, 225
Ross Revenge, MV 120
Royal Oak, HMS 148
Royal Naval College, the 36, 213
Royal Naval Museum 213
Royal Navy 45, 57, 59, 97, 98, 99, 100–101, 106, 112, 114, 125,
        129–131, 139, 143, 150, 152, 185, 210, 225
Royal Observatory, Greenwich 207, 210
Royal Ocean Racing Club 139
Russell, John 82
Ryan, Loch 172

S

Sailing By 20, 47, 81– 83, 87, 92, 218, 221

Sandbanks 39, 41, 134

Sandwich, Mayor of 116

Sargent, Epes 218–219

Scapa Flow 147–148, 152–153

Seaman, Keith 78

Sedgemore, HM Frigate 119

Shackleton, Sir E H 174

Shakespeare, William 120, 220

Shannon, HMS 141

Semaphore, see Meteorological

Shannon, see Shipping Areas

Shipping Areas

    Bailey 17, 22, 32, 34–35, 40, 70, 72, 145–146

    Biscay 16, 22, 32, 34–35, 40, 65, 132–133

    Cromarty 17, 32, 34–35, 40, 65, 67, 69–70, 71, 74, 99–100

    Dogger 17, 21, 32, 33, 34–35, 39, 65, 68, 69, 70–72, 74, 77,
        102–107

    Dover 17, 22, 29, 32, 34–35, 40, 56, 69, 70, 71, 110–121, 126,
        127, 134, 160

    Faeroes 16, 17, 32, 34–35, 40, 67, 69, 72, 146–148, 149

    Fair Isle 16, 17, 22, 32, 34–35, 40, 67, 146

    Fastnet 17, 32, 34–35, 40, 66, 68, 70, 137, 138–140

    Finisterre 22, 29, 33, 34–35, 69, 70, 71, 72, 134

    Fisher 17, 32, 34–35, 39, 67, 68, 69, 70, 73

    FitzRoy 16, 17, 29–30, 33, 39, 77, 134

    Forth 17, 32, 65, 67, 71, 98, 100–101

    Forties 17, 21, 32, 33, 34–35, 39, 69, 73, 93, 98–99, 148

    German Bight 17, 21, 33, 34–35, 40, 67, 68, 70, 71, 74, 77, 79,
        107–108

    Hebrides 17, 22, 32, 33, 34–35, 40, 69, 70, 72, 77, 144–145

Heligoland 33, 105, 107

Humber 17, 22, 32, 34–35, 40, 56, 69, 71, 79, 108

Irish Sea 17, 32, 34–35, 40, 66, 68, 69, 70, 71, 138, 140–141, 218

Lundy 17, 22, 32, 34–35, 40, 66, 68, 69, 70, 71, 134–137

Malin 17, 22, 32, 34–35, 40, 68, 69, 70, 143–144

Plymouth 17, 22, 32, 34–35, 56, 71, 129–132, 138–139, 219

Portland 17, 22, 32, 34–35, 40, 56, 70, 95, 129, 166

Rockall 17, 22, 32, 34–35, 40, 67, 68, 69, 70–72, 77, 142–143, 145,146

Shannon 17, 21, 32, 34–35, 40, 71, 141

Sole 16, 17, 22, 32, 34–35, 39, 134

South East Iceland 16, 20, 22, 40, 56, 67, 72, 94, 146, 151, 153

Thames 17, 22, 32, 34–35, 40, 56, 65, 69, 71, 79, 95, 96, 98, 109–110, 157, 207

Utsire 21, 33, 40, 68, 72, 73, 74, 97-98

Trafalgar 16, 17, 40, 56, 71, 94, 133

Tyne 17, 21, 32, 34–35, 40, 65, 67, 68, 69, 101–102

Viking 16, 17, 21, 33, 34–35, 39, 56, 69, 71, 73, 94–97

Wight 17, 22, 32, 34–35, 40, 56, 67, 70, 71, 93, 122–129

Shoreham 123

Signals, see Meteorological

Skaggerak 97

Smeaton, John 163–164

Smith's Knoll Light Vessel 41

Smith-Cumming, Sir G 183

Soanes, Zeb 76

Sole, see Shipping Areas

South East Iceland, see Shipping Areas

South Utsire, see Shipping Areas

Southampton, HMS 100

Spanish Armada 114, 115, 129

Stevenson, sons 161, 175

Stevenson, Robert Louis 160–164

Street, Sean 18, 67
Sunday Express, the 135
Supercomputers, see Meteorological
Sutors of Cromarty 99

T

Thames, see Shipping Areas
Time, see Meteorological
Times, the, 44, 217
Titanic, 101, 124, 145, 153, 182
Torch, Sidney, 82
Torrey Canyon, supertanker, 130–131, 132
Trade, the Board of, 24, 37, 44
Trafalgar, Battle of 125
Trafalgar, see Shipping Areas
Trinity House 41, 156–159, 163–164, 169–172, 182
Tyne, see Shipping Areas

U

U-Boats 31, 98, 100, 113, 132, 143, 147–148
UNHCR 74, 225
Utsire, see Shipping Areas

V

Versailles, Peace Treaty 148
Victory, HMS 125
Vidal, John 142

Viking, see Shipping Areas
Villeneuve, Admiral Pierre 133

W

Walmer 111, 115, 117, 118
Watson Dyson, Sir F 209
Wellington, Duke of 115, 130
Western Electric 208
Whild, Oscar, Lieutenant Commander 125
Wight, see Shipping Areas
Williams, Gwyneth 217
Wilson, Harold 131
Winstanley, Henry 162

Y

Yeovilton, RNAS 139
York, HMS 160

Z

Zeebrugge 127–128
Zeebrugge Raid 113